Naomi Zacharias is an extraordinarily talented writer, with the elegance and style of her father, Ravi, and the nurturing soul and strength of a woman. If this book doesn't cause you to weep at man's inhumanity toward man and woman, nothing else will. It is a stark reminder that without instruction from God, we are prone to a default mode of debauchery and sin that traps the less powerful in a cycle of self-loathing, poverty, abuse, and violence. But the stories in this book also give us hope that we can be the face, voice, and hands of God to those who have suffered from the worst that Adam's race has wrought.

LAUREN GREEN
chief religion correspondent
for Fox News Channel

Naomi Zacharias takes us on an eloquent, page-turning tour of abject human suffering, giving us an intimate view of physical, mental, and emotional despair on a level we can barely comprehend. As she relates the painful stories of others, she leads us on a parallel track, describing her own personal struggles and heartaches. Instead of impeding her goal to help others, the very hardships she was experiencing empowered her to empathize with them. It was through losing herself in the suffering of others that Naomi found herself, and through witnessing the sheer triumph of spirit in people who converted agonizing experiences into unquenchable flames of service that she discovered the boundlessness of God's grace. For when God is in charge, there is hope for the seemingly hopeless, hope that can flourish with just a "scent" of God's promise of redemption.

In *The Scent of Water*, Naomi shows us the truth of James 1:2–4: "Consider it pure joy, my brothers and sisters, whenever you face trials of many kinds, because you know the testing of your faith produces perseverance. Let perseverance finish its work so that you may be mature and complete, not lacking anything."

DAVID LIMBAUGH
nationally syndicated columnist and
author of *Crimes against Liberty*

the scent of water

grace for every kind of broken

naomi zacharias

ZONDERVAN®

ZONDERVAN.com/
AUTHORTRACKER
follow your favorite authors

ZONDERVAN

The Scent of Water
Copyright © 2010 by Naomi Zacharias

This title is also available as a Zondervan ebook. Visit www.zondervan.com/ebooks.

This title is also available in a Zondervan audio edition. Visit www.zondervan.fm.

Requests for information should be addressed to:

Zondervan, *Grand Rapids, Michigan 49530*

Library of Congress Cataloging-in-Publication Data

Zacharias, Naomi.
    The scent of water : grace for every kind of broken / Naomi Zacharias.
        p.   cm.
    Includes bibliographical references.
    ISBN 978-0-310-32737-0 (hardcover)
        1. Zacharias, Naomi. 2. Christian biography. 3. Church work with women.
    4. Christian life. I. Title.
    BR1725.Z32A3   2010
    253.092 — dc22   2010040113

All Scripture quotations, unless otherwise indicated, are taken from *The Holy Bible, English Standard Version*, copyright © 2001 by Crossway Bibles, a division of Good News Publishers. Used by permission. All rights reserved.

Any Internet addresses (websites, blogs, etc.) and telephone numbers printed in this book are offered as a resource. They are not intended in any way to be or imply an endorsement by Zondervan, nor does Zondervan vouch for the content of these sites and numbers for the life of this book.

All rights reserved. No part of this publication may be reproduced, stored in a retrieval system, or transmitted in any form or by any means — electronic, mechanical, photocopy, recording, or any other — except for brief quotations in printed reviews, without the prior permission of the publisher.

Published in association with the literary agency of Wolgemuth & Associates, Inc.

Cover design: Laura Maitner-Mason
Cover photography: Veer®
Interior design: Beth Shagene

Printed in the United States of America

11 12 13 14 15 /DCI/ 22 21 20 19 18 17 16 15 14 13 12 11 10 9 8 7 6 5 4 3 2 1

For Sarah,
who has always believed that I could —
whether it was in my ability to write pages worth reading
or to live a life worth anything,
you offered a faith that allowed me to borrow
from its graceful abundance

For there is hope for a tree,
    if it be cut down, that it will sprout again,
    and that its shoots will not cease.
Though its root grow old in the earth
    and its stump die in the soil,
yet at the scent of water it will bud
    and put out branches like a young plant.

JOB 14:7–9

contents

foreword

*An individual has not started living until he can rise
above the narrow confines of his individualistic concerns
to the broader concerns of all humanity.*
DR. MARTIN L. KING JR.

As a youngster, I was known to do one of two things with the allowance money I received from my mother, Mrs. Coretta Scott King. The first thing was to give the money to one of my classmates at Galloway School who was less fortunate than I. The second is still a source of laughs at family gatherings today. Devoid of a purse or pockets to hold my money, I would throw it (usually the Sunday morning offering my mom gave me) into the nearest trash can when I grew tired of holding it in my hands. Whereas the first act of benevolence is greeted with *awws* and nods of approval when shared, the second is always greeted with loud chuckles. Everyone except me knew that one of my cousins would always go behind me to collect what became his own personal offering. These two stories capture what I describe as haphazard benevolence. One act was purposive, as it spoke to who I was wired to be, even though I was too young to fully understand the impact; the other speaks to the ability of others to benefit from our accidental and unmitigated sharing, even when we did not intend or know we were doing it. In the end, through my haphazardness, all involved parties benefited (knowingly and unknowingly).

As I read Naomi Zacharias's *The Scent of Water*, I was deeply moved by what begins as well-researched, heartfelt, and brave frontline efforts to deliver hope and sustenance to God's children around the world. It ends *in a way that only God can bring about*: the author as the unsuspecting beneficiary of the haphazard benevolence of Annie's "authenticity" and Giovanni's wisdom. Whether on the streets of Amsterdam, in a prison in Cape Town, or in a café in Siena, Naomi's journey shows that "once you have been made aware, you have a responsibility to care." As a modern-day prophet, she passionately reminds us that "an individual has not started living until he can rise above the narrow confines of his individualistic concerns to the broader concerns of all humanity."

In an age when people kill each other over respect, we have lost sight of the great commission in Philippians 4:8: "Finally, brothers, whatever is true, whatever is noble, whatever is right … — if anything is excellent or praiseworthy — think about such things." Excellent and praiseworthy things are seen in Wellspring's ability to provide financial relief, second chances, and even vegetables for the least of God's children around the world. Moreover, we are taken on a journey of one woman's personal pain, which ultimately is healed through the reciprocal act of Christlike giving on the part of both Naomi and the wounded healers. The beauty in the symbiotic nature of the power of agape love — a cornerstone component of this book — is best echoed in a letter my father penned from a Birmingham jail cell in 1963: "We are caught in an inescapable network of mutuality, a single garment of destiny. What affects one directly, affects all indirectly." It becomes clear here that our "network of mutuality," which "affects all indirectly," must lead to a shift of perspective and a response to the clarion call for the body of Christ and global citizens to rise up and work to ameliorate the exploitation and gross abuse of people worldwide.

DR. BERNICE A. KING, last-born daughter of
Dr. Martin Luther King Jr. and Mrs. Coretta Scott King

prologue

the empty beach

I was twenty-seven when I first read the story about the Hasidic rabbi who told his people that if they studied the Torah, it would put Scripture on their hearts. A woman asked him, "But why *on* our hearts instead of *in* them?" The rabbi answered, "Only God can put Scripture inside. But reading sacred text can put it on your hearts, and then when your hearts break, the holy words will fall inside."

After reading the story, I folded down the corner of the page and placed my book on the small coffee shop table in front of me. I curled up in the oversized plum-colored velvet chair and slowly lifted the coffee cup to my lips as I contemplated the rabbi's words. It offered an explanation, a justification that I wanted to claim.

—

Sometimes I wake up in the morning, and before I open my eyes to take in the light of dawn, I wonder if perhaps it was a dream. Had my life really taken such an unscripted course? Had I really not been able to restore the situation by sheer willpower? After all, that's what I had always done before. It's who I was — someone with tenacity and unwavering faith in life itself.

Standing at the top of a mountain, I fell backward, descending past various arms of jutting rock that could be my rescue and perhaps bear my body's weight. But when I reached out to grab hold, the rock disintegrated in my hands. There was no rescue; nor was there the relief of actually hitting the ground. When you hit bottom, even rock-bottom, at least it's a destination. But this was an agonizing state of perpetual falling. No tangible place, nothing to remind me of who I was. It was the kind of dream you typically wake up from and have those moments of anxiety, only to be followed by indescribable relief when you realize it was not real. You find your bearings, sink back down onto your pillow, and pull the covers tightly under your chin.

On those particular mornings, with my eyes still closed, I want to believe I will wake up to a different life. It is not relief that fills me when my thoughts clear and the light of awareness cuts in. It always takes me several blinks to process it again. And then after several moments, I let out a sigh of resignation rather than determination, eventually turn back the covers, lower my bare feet to the floor, and step into the day again.

———

I was relieved that no one at this coffee shop knew me, or my thoughts and the fear and fatigue that simmered inside. My eyes wandered down to my left hand and the naked finger reminding me of what I was and what I wasn't.

The world went silent one day. It was noticeable, like the moment when you walk outside of a loud restaurant where you've been yelling at uncharted decibels in order to be heard by companions. Stepping outside of this world ringing with activity and energy, you are aware of the shocking quiet, the stillness around you.

I remember the exact moment I heard silence.

I felt like an observer, merely watching as life happened to others. For me, I saw only something blank and dark that seemed quite full of debris, but no sign of the rescue team that would swoop in, lower the lifeline, and coordinate the mass cleanup in an effort to remove all signs of the tragedy that had taken place.

In February 2005, I stood on the beach of Banda Aceh, Indonesia, just six weeks after the tsunami. Eeriness surrounded me as I watched the waves break placidly just feet away, the smooth waters trickling up the beach before lazily falling back down. The sun was out, beating down on the black head covering and long black sleeves I wore in observance of Shari'a law, the Islamic law of the land. The weight of my knee-high black rubber boots reminded me of each step I took, and I adjusted my face mask in a useless effort to feel a little less constricted.

I arrived at this beach exhausted and somewhat disoriented after long hours in non-air-conditioned airplane cabins, enduring countless connections and flights during all hours of multiple nights to try to get to a place no one could get to. Traveling with three colleagues in international humanitarian work and a videographer, we eventually made it to the last stop of our journey. My colleagues and I had formed a consortium to create a support effort in response to the natural disaster, and so we embarked on this mission together.

Transported by a military cargo plane, courtesy of the Indonesian navy, we landed on a small airstrip in the province of Banda Aceh on the island of Sumatra. We were escorted by local military police to a temporary office, where we waited for ages while they carefully examined each page of our passports, emphatically stressed the importance of our head coverings, issued badges that authorized us as humanitarian aid workers, and — finally — granted access to this area that had been most severely hit by the tsunami. While we waited, I wandered around the office, stepping up to a wall that had numerous charts, diagrams, and lists. There I found the posted body recovery for each day since tragedy struck the island on December 26, 2004. I lifted a finger to locate yesterday's number and followed the line to the right side of the page ... 582.

Pictures of missing family members were haphazardly taped to the wall by desperate loved ones who were still clinging to the unlikely hope that those pictured would be safely rescued or at least identified. A photo of a little boy with round dark eyes and pursed lips grabbed my attention. I had never seen this little boy before, and yet somehow I felt his loss deep within me as I found myself unable to look away from his picture. I wondered what his name was, how many birthdays he had celebrated, what his voice sounded like. It was barely noon on the fifty-first day of rescue and recovery, and the report in Aceh would ultimately confirm that more than 160,000 lives had been lost.

Finally we were cleared to begin our exploration. Two officers in military fatigues, with machine guns slung over their shoulders, remained with us throughout the day in an effort to provide security in a suddenly very unstable place. Rebel factions had fired fatal shots hours before, and the Indonesian government was making every effort to ensure the safety of foreign aid workers. Our new shadows looked intimidating, but they offered reassuring glances as we uncertainly began on our way. Only moments later, we slowly drove past the first of countless freshly hollowed mass graves we would see that day, truckloads of remains waiting to be callously lowered inside these coffins of earth.

This tsunami reportedly released energy equivalent to 23,000 Hiroshima-type atomic bombs, making it arguably the most destructive scientifically documented natural disaster in history. It happened suddenly, but it wasn't a single event. Rather, it was the result of a trail of unforeseen occurrences, each one leading to the full path of destruction.

For countless years, the sliding of a section of the earth's crust called the India plate had been pressing against the Burma plate. Each plate pushed relentlessly against the other, refusing to yield or call a truce. And so, as with all tugs-of-war, eventually something had to give in order to create, or commandeer, space. As the India and Burma plates engaged in their battle, the need for space finally proved to be the greatest force, and the earth itself responded with violent spasms. When this event happens within the earth, we call it *a natural disaster.*

When disaster happens in our own lives, we accept it as anything but natural and spend sleepless nights and countless dollars on therapy to try to define exactly what went wrong and why. I think, in part, we long for it to be quantified because this will validate our own personal sense of loss and pain.

Wouldn't it be easier to say, "I just registered a 7.8 on the Heartache Scale"? There would be no need for further explanation, and everyone could understand exactly what you had suffered. But we have no such measuring stick and often feel isolated by disappointment and loss we can't describe.

Worse still are the interactions with those who know just a portion of the story and offer their expert opinions on exactly what went wrong. The perceived error they confidently pinpoint as the cause more often than not just leaves us further confused and unsure of our own step. But any human tragedy is rarely so simple and is instead frequently the result of a sequence of events that led to the catastrophic outcome. We long for scientific terms and numbers to classify the shattered hopes, the level of calamity, the survey of damage, that would seem to give respect to the gravity of the tragedy, and we seek some type of formula for repair with measures to ensure it will never happen again.

———

The seismic activity created by the plate shift–induced earthquake registered 9.3 out of 10 on the Richter Scale. A 10 describes an earthquake of epic proportions and has never been recorded in history. But the conversation was not yet over. In response to the earthquake, tumultuous shock waves unfurled in chaos across 3,000 miles of the Indian Ocean in eleven countries, from Indonesia to Africa. In Banda Aceh, wave heights reportedly reached 50 feet and sped inland at a speed of more than 90 miles an hour. Initial reports delivered the news that 68,000 lives had been lost. Days later, the official report listed the toll at more than 250,000.

These are the facts, and from here we always have the choice — to walk away and only feel a dutiful amount of sympathy and recognition that this was, in fact, a terrible thing, or to venture inside, to look at the people, the places, and the soul of what was lost. But we know that once we walk through this door, we will not emerge the same. It's impossible to truly engage in significant loss without losing part of ourselves in the process.

In retrospect, I think it was the opportunity to lose something of myself that drew me here in the first place. Stepping out of the truck, I felt the wave of heat from the temperature that soared to more than 100 degrees. But it wasn't the heat that made me feel breathless. I looked around me and tried to comprehend the complete and utter devastation. As far as the eye could see, there was ... nothing. Debris at knee-high levels obstructed every possible path as we stepped over a stray blue shoe, pieces of tattered clothing, and beams that once supported a house — signs that there had been life, and reminders that it was gone. It was impossible to tell where there had been a road, or a yard, or the front door of a building. There were no houses, no buildings, and no trees, not one living thing growing out of the ground. A crew of rescue workers walked past us in jumpsuits and helmets, carrying a bright orange body bag and the lost life it contained. Laying it in the bed of a white truck, it rested among countless others recovered that morning.

As my colleagues and I continued toward the waterfront, a portion of a wall from a house stood alone among the rubble. Someone had used black spray paint to issue an urgent plea in harsh, uneven letters:

YA ALLAH KAMI BERTOBAT.
YA ALLAH TOLONG SELAMAT KANIKAMI TUHAN.

I looked expectantly at my Indonesian colleague to translate. "Dear Lord, we confess. Lord, save us from this disaster," he quietly uttered as he walked away.

In describing the tsunami, the reports explained that the water drew back severely, exposing great lengths of ocean floor. Onlookers stared in confusion. Some ran into the ocean bed to recover fish and floundering sea life, excited by the opened treasure chest. Others began running in the opposite direction, for the exposed floor seemed ominous. Then in a surreal moment, the churning waters unleashed that initial wave that soared to 50 feet, raged at breakneck speed, and angrily crashed over a mile inland. Flooding the land, it ripped houses apart and pulled at the arms of terrified men and women desperately clinging to trees and mistaken strongholds.

As we stood on the beach, the water seemed so harmless now. It was hard to imagine the destruction it had inflicted. The beach was supposed to be beautiful, and it would have been, under different circumstances. But all that surrounded it was mass destruction and fragments of life. There were no children playing on the beach, no sounds of distant laughter. There was no music. There was nothing.

Silence — except for the faint sound of sobbing.

As I walked toward the lone sound in a lost abyss, I came upon a woman standing alone on the beach. She stood back at a distance, her bare feet balancing herself on large rocks that protruded from the sand. She looked to be in her forties, and her brown skin was weathered from the sun, and perhaps from life itself. She wore a black jilbab, an Islamic head covering, though rebellious wisps of hair had succumbed to the breeze and escaped its hold. Her left arm dangled in an unnatural way by her side, and the angst in her face was palpable. But what I remember most was her eyes. They were a striking color of hazel, the kind that you can't take your gaze from because of their unusual and riveting shade. They pierced my soul then and held me captive. Not because of their obvious beauty, but because of the utter and indescribable pain they imparted.

She wailed unashamedly and cried out in Bahasa, the native language whose words I could not understand but whose tones of pleading I could not mistake. I waved my friend over to translate for me again, and through trembling sobs she could not control, the woman spoke of her two children. She had desperately tried to hold on to the small hands of her six- and eight-year-old daughters, but the force of the water was no match for even a mother's supernaturally charged protection. Her left arm was dislocated in the process, but she had refused to leave the shore where she had last seen her daughters' faces, even for the relief of medical attention. I don't think she felt the pain from her arm at all. And she knew that the clinic could do absolutely nothing for the true source of her agony.

It seemed impossible for beauty and undeniable devastation to exist in exactly the same space. Her eyes were lovely and had a lifetime of stories to reveal, but could now only speak of one story. I could not reply, for no words seemed to provide an adequate response to her tragedy. A trite response about loss and the will of God lacked clarity and a satisfying answer even to me. And yet I could think of no thoughtful word to offer true solace either. I didn't know what to say, what to hope for, or what she was going to do. My gaze wandered as I inwardly searched for an answer.

As I looked away for a few moments, I saw at a distance another portion of a wall. I squinted to make out the painted words:

PEMILIK RUMAHINI MASIH HIDUP TSUNAMI
26 DEC 2004.

"The owner of this house survived the tsunami on December 26, 2004."

———

Certain kinds of beauty are easy to recognize. Others require a careful eye, and when uncovered, much beauty lies in the story itself. In a special edition on world wonders, *Life* magazine told of another collision that took place eons ago. The continent of India crept northward, eventually running into the giant landmass of Asia. Among the ramifications of this colossal impact was something that would eventually be given a Sanskrit name: the Himalayas. The world's tallest and most famous mountain was birthed, and people around the globe would marvel at the fortitude, foreboding mystery, and sheer beauty of Mount Everest.

Perhaps the distinguishing moment of any catastrophe is not found in the fracture itself. Perhaps what distinguishes any one disaster from another is not what has been lost, but what survives.

The truth was, I honestly didn't know what had survived.

chapter 1

great expectations

When I was little, I sat in red flannel pajamas with footies, curled up next to my mother as she read to me the stories of Cinderella, Sleeping Beauty, and Snow White. I listened intently as my mind was captivated by the wonders of fairy godmothers with magical wands, adorable mice, and battles waged against evil and envy and all that was ugly in life. My eyes widened every time good triumphed over evil (in the end), the hero always got his girl, and they lived happily ever after.

As my dreams began to take shape, I, too, believed that life would turn out as it seemed it should: that darkness and evil would not prevail over the "happily ever after" that was mine. And when my life did not turn out the way it was supposed to, I felt I had been played for a fool. Life was certainly no fairy tale, and although cynicism was an obvious escape from the ache, I could not quite commit to it. I nostalgically looked back to the time, the hope, when I believed that life would imitate the storybook.

Modern-day fairy tales don't tell us the real story. They don't even tell us the rest of the story. They don't tell us what happens when the prince does not show up in time, or how to endure the potency of a poisonous apple. *The End* often appears in cursive at the point that the real story would begin. It is what nearly breaks the protagonists, what sometimes *does* break them, that is the real story. But it is not one for the faint of heart.

I felt great animosity for my own life, and when I referred to it with disloyalty one day, my father quietly said, "The shortest route is not always the best route." And when I was discouraged by the recognition that I had only a flawed story to offer to another, he released me into a truth: "There are no such fairy tale loves. The garden of Eden proved that," he wrote to me. "Love has to battle through. In fact, if it has never had to, one wonders if it can be true."

I can't be alone in longing for the fairy-tale life, and as I read the stories, I realized that perhaps we should all be careful what we wish for. To my surprise, as I fed my fairy-tale obsession and buried myself in research of famous narratives, I discovered it was not the fairy tales that had failed me. Clearly we have since watered them down to minimize the decidedly uncomfortable, but the original fairy tales actually affirmed my father's words to me. They were filled with lions and tigers and very grown-up darkness that actually offered critical insight into life.

In the 1800s, the Brothers Grimm published their story of Sleeping Beauty, which began with the birth of a beautiful baby girl. To share their excitement, her parents, the king and queen of a land far, far away, threw the grandest of parties. But they made a critical mistake when they forgot to invite a certain fairy to the celebration, and the scorned fairy retaliated by placing a curse on their child: *At the age of sixteen, she will prick her finger and die.*

A good fairy was not able to erase the curse, but she could alleviate the ultimate of horrors. Instead of death, the prick of her finger would incite a deep, deep sleep. The better of the curses also allowed for an escape clause: A love, *true love*, that was pure could awaken her. Thankfully, Sleeping Beauty was lucky enough to be awakened by such a true kiss, and all was as good as new. Or was it? She had been sleeping, waiting, and under the curse for *one hundred years*. During that time, her mother died from a broken heart and her fairy advocate twiddled the entire kingdom into a deep sleep to try to preserve some semblance of her life should the princess ever awaken. There was suffering — and not hers alone.

Ariel lost her majestic voice. Rapunzel wandered aimlessly in a desert wasteland for years in misery while the prince and father of her children was rendered blind and did "naught but lament and weep" over the loss of his wife. Cinderella was first orphaned, then enslaved before she tried on the glass slipper that changed her world.

We want the good part of the fairy tale, the culmination of all things good; and with such idealism, we have only preserved the idea of *happily ever after*. On the screen and in our minds we have rewritten the stories and forgotten about the battles the heroines chose to fight. The resolve is only significant because of the magnitude of the darkness. It required a love and justice that were extraordinary to redeem what had gone so awfully wrong. The love that was grand is powerfully intoxicating. But we have chosen to overlook the pain and the price that the players paid to find it.

The flaw is not in the stories themselves or in the restoration they portray. The flaw is in the happily ever after, since real life does not always end in such a way. Yet of even this fantasy we were carefully warned. The Grimm's Brothers' conclusion of *Sleeping Beauty* provided a caution: "They lived happily ever after, as they always do in fairy tales, not quite so often, however, in real life." It was the only disclaimer, the distinction made between real life and fantasy, for the rest remained quite realistic.

In his book *Orthodoxy*, G. K. Chesterton penned a chapter he cleverly titled "The Ethics of Elfland," in which he claimed there are two requirements for every fairy tale.[1] The first — one he calls the doctrine of conditional joy — is the necessity of the "if." *If* you don't return by midnight, the coach will go back to being an ordinary pumpkin. The second rule is what Chesterton calls the fairy godmother philosophy: The condition stipulated cannot be questioned. He further explains that no one can ever ask the fairy godmother, "How come?" — for to do so, he warns, would only beg another question. To ask, "How is it that I must leave the ball at twelve?" the fairy godmother could rightfully answer, "How is it that you are *going* there until twelve?" The rule is essentially this familiar bit of clichéd advice: "Don't look a gift horse in the mouth." In the case of fairy tales, we cannot require an explanation for the supernatural. The acceptance of the inexplicable is simply the way it works to be in the presence of miracles and mystery.

In real life, we would now do well not to draw our conclusions to an expectant close. When there is the chance of a miracle, but no guarantee of such, there will certainly be the alternate possibility of disappointment, fully explainable reality, and pain. This present world is not the best of all possible worlds. It is just the best of all possible *means* to the best of all possible worlds. Heaven is the happily ever after. Until then, we still live with frogs and century-long naps.

There is, however, a "once upon a time." There are evil and heartache. There are darkness and our own dragons to fight. There are not the likes of singing mice, but there are details equally miraculous. *More* miraculous.

I wanted to leave the familiar — my own evil and heartache — and find people who were the most vulnerable; to be where something was tragically broken that was not me. It was not to feel comforted by seeing the pain of another, but rather to feel another's pain. I needed to exist outside of my own. *Smooth and flawless* held nothing to comfort me, nothing to teach me, and nothing to fill me.

The reality is that I was running from something I could not fix, a self I could not forgive, and a story I could not accept.

This is a story; it is not *the* story, for no life can be characterized by a single story. It is one that I started to see unfold when I walked into an unlikely room to listen to the story of another. It is not neatly packaged. It is far from tidy. But I do not need the balm of cynicism to endure its pages. Because it has been significantly rich. And because it is mine.

In his biographical novel of Michelangelo, Irving Stone unveils a discussion between the young apprentice and his teacher, Bertoldo. "To try to understand another human being, to grapple for his ultimate depths, that is the most dangerous of human endeavors," the instructor counseled as he brushed strokes of wisdom on his student.[2]

So I start with the ever-important beginning that is mine and yours to claim.

Once upon a time ...

chapter 2

objects of fantasy

Once upon a time, I walked into a brothel and met a girl named Annie. I was not there by accident, but it was not a room I deliberately set out to find either.

I had been nervous the last time I was there as I walked down those narrow cobblestone streets, aware of the dark shadows against the brick exteriors of buildings that were deceptively beautiful. But once inside the door, I stood in a dimly lit maze of sparsely furnished rooms that each contained a woman who was for sale.

The first time I saw Amsterdam's world-famous red-light district, I found myself unable to articulate intelligent sentences for the next several days. I had previously been to the brothel-lined streets in Mumbai, India, where over 70,000 women worked in prostitution. They were behind bars, eyes of chestnut and onyx piercing the shadows. The streets in Mumbai were dark and ominous, and there was a sense of something that should remain hidden.

In troublesome blazing contrast, the district streets of Amsterdam were filled with blinking neon lights so you couldn't miss a detail, even if you wanted to. There was laughter, a sense of overt celebration. An old church sat empty and quiet near its center, a haunting suggestion that perhaps life here hadn't always been this way. Loud music filled my ears; fountains were lit with floodlights; bouncers tried aggressively to direct me into bars and theaters. Four hundred windows lined the streets, each with a red light overhead and a woman behind it for sale. They were all ages, including young girls whose papers claimed they were the legal age of eighteen but whose baby-smooth skin and wide eyes suggested otherwise. There were also women in their sixties who had worked there for years, a lifetime of standing behind their windows each night, waiting to be chosen and paid. The women were arranged like products in a store, each nationality on a particular aisle, as it were. To find girls from Africa, head to one end of the street. All of the girls from Hungary were on the next corner. I felt waves of nausea swirling inside me.

I was there to meet Toos, a woman who would quickly become my friend. She is the director of an organization called Scarlet Cord. Based in the red-light district, they are advocates for women both personally and legally and provide resources, counseling, and financial support to offer an option for a woman who wants to leave prostitution to be able to do so. They do not coerce; they do not use tactics of guilt. Their identified goal of liberating her to have an alternative is grounded in the belief that she is created by God and has intrinsic value that cannot be stripped from her and ought not to be exploited. The mission is not to tell a woman that prostitution is wrong and bring her out of sin; it is not to tell her all the things she is not. The mission is to affirm *who she is.*

Toos makes regular visits into the district each week. She knocks on the windows to introduce herself to girls working in the brothels. She leaves a business card and oftentimes a Bible or literature telling the true story of a girl who one day left the district for good. Over time, she builds a relationship with them, and icy expressions are transformed into sincere smiles when they see her familiar face. She walks through the streets boldly and without fear, seemingly oblivious to the looks her beauty draws from men. She is there for the women, and her focus is entirely on them.

———

Walking around the district, I expected to see men who looked disturbed, who looked like they belonged in such a dark place. Instead, I saw attractive men of all ages and nationalities. I saw fathers with their junior high–aged boys, pointing in this direction and that, seemingly giving a lesson about the way things work in this other world that in reality is just a part of town. I heard a man on his cell phone explaining to his wife that he was caught in traffic and would be home late that evening. I pushed through gatherings of guys and ignored their comments, pausing to glare at them with angrily offended eyes. There were four hundred women available to them, albeit unfortunately, but even that wasn't enough, and they behaved inappropriately to any woman they saw who was not available to them. Behavior they wouldn't consider displaying if we had passed each other on the street five blocks away was demonstrated without the slightest hint of embarrassment in this all-permissive zone. It was supposed to represent freedom. So why was it that, as a woman, I felt anything but liberated?

I looked up to see a group of college-aged American guys laughing gregariously, high-fiving each other in congratulations after their latest conquest before they descended into a dingy theater where their eyes and minds would be filled with images of men, women, and sexuality reduced to something that exploited and demeaned all three objects and the viewers simultaneously. They believed they were there to use the women, and they were right.

I didn't know where to look, for as each woman stood with her body exposed behind a window, I did not want to disrespect her by looking. But I didn't want to disrespect her by pretending she was not there. I do not think many passersby stopped to look into her eyes, the lenses that looked out from a soul inside. No, it is easier to pretend she does not have one. I saw the large tattoo on an upper arm, another on the left hip, of a girl a few windows down. They were the symbols of her pimp, a type of branding to signify that she was owned. Each telltale design served to alert other pimps that she was not available to them, for her body was the property of another.

Back in the dark room of a brothel, I spoke with one of the girls, and she rolled her dark-blue eyes in disgust at the men. She spoke of their foolishness, their ignorance, and how simple it was to extract more money from them. "Particularly those American men," she scoffed. She believed she was there to use the men, and she was right.

Some of the girls were hardened. Some were clearly frightened. Some were visibly bruised. Some were angry. They were all affected. As I took in the whole scene, I was deeply saddened, for this was a place where every participant was asked to be less than they are.

I am always a bit confused when people ask me about a particular girl I speak of. They casually ask if she "chose" prostitution. If I note that she was not trafficked, there is a visible shift in their eyes and in their interest. *This one is not our problem*, body language seems to say as we draw conclusions about the woman who was trafficked and the one who is there "by choice." The inference is that a woman who is there by choice has, in effect, created her own circumstance. It becomes easy to wash our hands of her and judge her, affixing our own ID label to her person.

The distinction offers a technical explanation, but the application becomes problematic — in part, because as the details were exposed in story after story, I was not sure there was any real choice for any of those girls. If the same things had happened to me, I think I would be standing on the same side of the window. In any event, *how* she got there did not alter my reaction to her present circumstance. Someone's willingness to subject herself to something has never made a harmful act any less exploitive or relieved the offender of responsibility. If this were so, then neither should we intervene on behalf of the abused wife who chooses to endure beatings or the laborer who willingly goes to work in the sweatshop because he needs an income in order to eat.

The reality that we live in is rarely as simple as we want it to be.

Once upon a time, people believed the world was flat. I can't help but wonder if this perception would never have originated in the East, where a texture beyond topography is attributed to life.

You could say that my father gave me the world. It wasn't a snow globe that I could shake to watch the magic of glittery snowflakes gracefully falling on a city contained safely inside a glass bubble. It was not a present he brought back to tell me he remembered me while away on a business trip. It could not be unwrapped on Christmas morning or after blowing out the candles on a chocolate birthday cake.

He opened up the world by living in a way that invited me,

that implored me even, to see the perspective found through his eyes. Past their Indian shade of darkest brown lay a window to a world that could never be flat. It was too grand, too complex, too rich, and I could never exhaust its layers. It lay at my fingertips, within my reach and outside of my grasp. From the time I was a little girl, I believed in a metaphorical wardrobe that would allow me to enter the depths of somewhere.

When my father taught me how to see texture in a world outside of myself, neither of us could have foreseen that he would have to help me through the growing pains of seeing texture in the world *within* me as well. Ever true to fluidity, the two converged and offered me perspective, each one into the other. It could not be granted in a single day or experience, but rather as a perpetual offering that I have had to embrace again and again in an effort to accept both the world to which I am bound and a world I choose to venture into.

My older sister tells me how, as a six-year-old, she would lay awake in bed wondering what she could do to protect us if an intruder broke into our home. It never occurred to me that this could happen, much less to worry about what I would do about it. I had a strong will, and my worries never traveled very far, because if I set my mind to it, I could "fix" anything. It's who I was.

When I was confronted with a problem I could not fix, I was left with not just the loss of something that meant something to me, but the loss of who I thought I was. And so I wanted to try to do for another what I could not do for myself.

Ironically, I chose to enter a world of extreme tragedy that had problems far beyond what I could ever fix.

One week before my twenty-sixth birthday, I accepted a job opportunity that enabled me to pursue a personal compulsion to be involved in human rights and humanitarian initiatives. I was young and naive, and many people would not have hired me for the job. But my father chose to put unwarranted faith in me in spite of likely advice to the contrary, and he believed I could help launch a new venture called Wellspring International to research global needs for women and children at risk and to develop a process of due diligence to evaluate organizations seeking to meet those needs. Our mission was to facilitate financial support to meet such needs by providing donors with confidence that their gifts were managed with integrity and were meeting legitimate purposes.

During the first year, my goal was to absorb a wealth of information from attorneys, donors, the media, and organizations working overseas. When I delved into global issues of abuse and exploitation, I discovered the dark underbelly of humanity. I suppose I knew this going into it, but a statistic is always different from a face; hearing a woman's voice convert to reality as she utters her real name is different from seeing her persona through an anything-but-transparent window.

People often ask if it is difficult to sit down and talk with the girls in the red-light district because my story is different in its details. I find it interesting that we ask this of ourselves and of each other, because I have never been asked this by one of the girls I talked to. Rather than the differences in our stories, what is overwhelmingly apparent are the things that are the same and the things that would certainly be the same if our past experiences were exchanged.

It was about ten o'clock one crisp winter night, and I was back in Amsterdam to accompany Toos on her regular visit into the red-light district. We had our coats zipped up to protect us against the December chill. It was Sinterklaas, the Dutch celebration of the Christmas season. Many people were at home, eating waffles with warm chocolate syrup and watching excited children unwrap gifts. But not everyone. For the streets of the red-light district had still drawn a notable crowd on a festive evening that is supposed to be filled with wishes and hopes, belief, and sugar-dipped doughnuts.

I was not nervous this time. Instead I was looking for familiar faces and did not know if I should feel fear or relief if I could not find them.

"Did you see that guy?" a female voice called out to us. She was standing outside her door, leaning over the railing and pointing just ahead of us. "He was walking around with a camera," she shook her head, still angry. "But I showed him," she said. "I poured a whole can of Sprite over his head!" She laughed as my friend and I exchanged dubious glances. We later learned that the recipient of the unwelcome soda shower was, as we feared, my cameraman. He was not recording in the district, but was carrying the equipment over his shoulder after taping interviews in Toos's office down the street. She and I looked at each other and didn't know whether to feel sorry for him or to laugh. We did decide, however, not to mention to her that we suspected we might know the perceived offender, and we quickly changed the subject and accepted the invitation to step inside her room.

The room was almost bare. There was nothing on the walls; the only piece of furniture was a metal frame with a thin twin mattress on top. We lowered ourselves against the wall to sit on the floor while she began to tell her story. Her name was Annie. At times she seemed like a fragile child, and just moments later like a rage-filled woman who knew her share of pain.

"I tell new girls three things," she explained. "Number one: a man will only ever hurt you. Number two: don't do drugs; it will only make things more complicated. And number three: always keep a can of petrol nearby so you can set them on fire if they give you trouble." I wondered if I was supposed to laugh, but realized she was serious.

The conversation then meandered around to her spiritual beliefs, which seemed to be a blend of Buddhism, Christianity, and her own conclusions: "I believe in God. I pray to him every night when I sit in the shower and try to wash away this dirty feeling. I pray he's there …"

"Have you considered going to church?" Toos asked.

Annie laughed softly and gave a pained smile. And then she took us back in time before bringing us forward.

Annie was working in an entry-level job for an airline at Changi International Airport on the island of Singapore when a Dutch passenger engaged her in conversation one day. Soon it seemed he came through often, and each time he did, he carried gifts for her. Shyly, she began to look forward to his visits. He showed an interest in her thoughts and her world. After nearly a year of airport romance, this charming man asked her to marry him. It had not been a typical courtship by any means, but when she told her family, they were thrilled and encouraged her to accept this opportunity. Love was not necessarily a consideration, and they were certain this would mean a better life for her.

So Annie married him and left her country, her parents, her brothers and sisters, her language, and all things familiar to go with her husband, a man still quite a bit the stranger as he took her to a foreign land. She was nervous but also felt anticipation. It was kind of like a fairy tale: a good-looking, exotic guy swooping her up to fly to a new place.

To her great disbelief, arrival in Amsterdam brought the end of life as she had known it. It was nothing she had dreamed of; in fact, it was a brutal nightmare that had no morning. Her husband held her passport and her license to go home and delivered her to a window. She did not speak Dutch, and with no papers to show where she was from or that she was even there legally, she did not go to the police. Her every move was commandeered by him. He did not allow her to communicate with her family, and with threats she was convinced he would make good on, Annie was helpless and very much alone. She was nineteen years old and lost. And no one was coming to rescue her.

Defeated and effectively silenced, Annie did what she never imagined she would do: she stood behind a window. As her pimp led a customer to her window, she turned off her soul with the downward flip of the switch to the red light above her door. She shuddered even as she told of the moment from years ago, vividly remembering the first trick that would leave her embittered and forever changed.

Over time she became pregnant, and still her husband insisted that she work. In a business where sex is king and a woman's body the means to this end, there is a market for every kind of perversion. She lost the baby when his anger at her lack of submission one day resulted in heavy and repeated blows to her stomach. She wanted that baby, the one hint of life in a body that felt otherwise dead.

At this point in her story, I saw a visible change in Annie's countenance and demeanor. The previously vulnerable tone was replaced with cold anger and a raw vengeance.

Six years into this life she abhorred, Annie learned that her mother had died. She had, of course, missed the funeral. This awakened the brewing rage within her, and she unleashed it by setting fire to her husband's car, somewhat crazily warning him that she would do the same to him if she had to. She didn't care anymore; she had nothing to lose. She wouldn't stand behind the window another night and didn't care what he did to her. She demanded her passport a final time.

Her husband had profited as he hoped. There were other girls, newer girls, and she was not worth this kind of trouble any longer. So with a shrug of his shoulders, he handed Annie her thin passport booklet, and she ran all the way home.

She told her family the whole story of all that had happened, but they did not respond with sorrow or compassion. They did not wrap their arms around her to shield her against the pain inflicted on her; they did not counter its degradation. They disowned her. Working in prostitution disgraced the family name, regardless of how or why she ended up there.

Annie leaned forward and said to us, "*This* ... this was the most painful thing that has ever happened to me. And so I returned to Amsterdam, because it is where I fit; it is what I am." By default, it had become home.

She returned to the street and worked for herself this time. Without a pimp, she made a decent income. But soon she began to long again for a different kind of life. She applied for a job at a factory and was immediately hired after the interview. She even went to church a few times. But one day someone at work recognized her, and the secret of her past life was revealed, leaving her ashamed and ostracized.

Like the story in the Bible, the male offender who could attest to her profession seemed to escape the judgment. Dutifully stoned by a jury of her peers, Annie had to leave her new job.

She looked at Toos and me intensely and asked, "You tell me.

If I were to walk into your church today, would people see me as a woman, or would they see me as a prostitute?"

I did not reply to her somewhat rhetorical question, because I wasn't sure I was proud of the answer. Toos answered with both the mature honesty and compassion she deserved. "Some would see you as a prostitute. But they would be wrong. And it is not how Jesus would see you."

Annie shook her head resolutely. "No," she said with conviction, the kind of conviction that only exists when an infinite depth of emotion is attached to it. "The problem with your people is, they tell me I should leave, but they never want to let me forget where I came from either."

I have never forgotten Annie's words about the church, as she was profoundly and tragically right. We do this to each other, and we do it to others ... like Annie. We sentence someone who is already wounded to prison, forever defined and bound by a label we slap on them, one they can never remove or replace in our eyes.

I liked Annie. When she appeared fragile and childlike, I wanted to hug her. When she was angry and said she often stared out at the canal and dreamed of pushing men into it to sentence them to the fatal death imposed on her internally, I wanted her to find a resurrection of her spirit. I wanted her to see herself the way I saw her. I couldn't fix anything, and I think if I had foolishly thought for even a second that I could, she would have rightfully thrown me in that canal too.

What Annie did require of me, though, was authenticity. As we spoke of disappointment and of life choices that invoke pain, she paused and studied me intently, wordlessly. I knew she was evaluating me, and I said nothing to her silent stare but simply held her gaze. After seconds, she looked at me with sincerity and said almost protectively, "So what did the a**hole do to you anyway?"

I smiled but said nothing. In my own world back home I felt uncomfortable and unknown, yet here was a woman whom I had met less than an hour before, and she managed to see in me something I had learned to hide. Somehow, this provided much-needed validation that what I felt was, in fact, legitimate. For some reason, this took away a fraction of the sting itself.

⌒

When Holland legalized prostitution in 2000, it was a win for women's rights; it was a vote for Annie. They said women would be entitled to more options and better working conditions. And 20,000 women began registered work as taxpaying civilians in what quickly became a place world-renowned for sex tourism.

Present-day women's rights activist Karina Schaapman formerly worked in prostitution and is now a member of the Amsterdam city council. When rumors of a dark past started to arise, notably because the father of one of her children's class-mates recognized her in the schoolyard, she decided to confront the rumors and wrote a book to tell her story. In *Motherless*, Schaapman recounted her experience working in the red-light district and soon became the point person for issues involving prostitution, a platform she had not expected to occupy when voted into office.

Schaapman investigated abuses in prostitution and released an official report in 2008 titled "Making the Invisible Visible." Her research found that 75 percent of the city of Amsterdam's 8,000 to 11,000 prostitutes were from Eastern Europe, Africa, and Asia. Criminologist Frank Bovenkerk released similar findings on behalf of the city of Amsterdam and in a separate publication released evidence that the majority of women working in the red-light district were forced into prostitution.

Pimping and brothels are allowed, but trafficking and violence are not. But the women do not file reports for various reasons, including legitimate fear for their own safety or that of their family. Law enforcement has knowledge of, and a portfolio of, nearly one hundred violent pimps, but they cannot prosecute them without the women's testimony. What was purported to be a ruling in favor of women's rights actually served to increase their vulnerability and exposed the city to organized crime and trafficking.

A world that boasts of freedom is, in reality, capitalizing on global poverty and human trade, creating a new prison for those who have already been victims in another sphere of life. Human beings are the commodities bought and sold, on both sides of the window.

Every year, millions of tourists visit the red-light district in Amsterdam. Some are there to witness the phenomenon with their own eyes; others are there to barter and purchase. There is always an older couple holding hands and looking through the windows. There is always an Asian tour guide holding up her sign and directing her group to follow. There are women out for girls' night, pointing and laughing. There are groups of young guys, and there are middle-aged men walking alone. It is somewhat inexplicable how normalized it became and still is. It's a crude business where women are for sale. I struggle to imagine another accepted world like it, where if human beings step onto the auction block, an audience would gather in fascination or curiosity. It doesn't just say something about Amsterdam, for Amsterdam only revealed something about the rest of the world.

chapter 3

the same side of the window

Elise was supposed to go to the store to buy a loaf of bread and three bottles of beer. Her mother had just enlisted her daughter's help to forcefully empty her stomach of its contents as she lay intoxicated on the sofa. It had not been a fun afternoon. And now, the girl didn't want to go to the store; she wanted to stay home and play a game or read a book. She wanted to do normal things.

She was nine years old.

But Elise's mother insisted, and so she buttoned up her cherry-red coat against the cool spring morning in the Czech Republic. The line at the market seemed like it would never end, and she hopped from one leg to the next in her boredom. Her arms were tired of holding on to the heavy bottles, and she wondered how she would ever make her way past the longer legs that kept pushing her farther back in the line. Her size and age were misleading. Childhood was not a luxury she had experienced.

When Elise was only a young teenager, her mother asked her to go to see her grandmother and steal some money again from the old woman. Elise was tired of stealing, and she hated betraying her grandmother. When she rounded the corner by her grandmother's apartment building, she caught sight of several teenage gang members. She immediately lowered her head and quickened her pace, but the boys would not be dissuaded. When she stepped into the lobby of her grandmother's building, they forced their way inside.

She tried to fight off the attackers, but they outnumbered her, and she could not protect her body against them. She simply was not strong enough. And so, to escape the horror, her mind did what her body could not. It fled to a place they could not reach, even while they raped her body, one by one. The boys disappeared, and she was alone. She pulled herself up, still hiding inside her mind, and stole from her grandmother to fulfill the objective of her visit.

Her body was scarred, the doctor told her. She would never bear children. But by the time she was eighteen, she had two small children. Neither father had stayed around, and she had lost her older child to social services.

Elise worked the night shift at a bar around the corner from home to support herself and her baby. She married again. Not for love, of course, but because with a husband she'd be able to care for her child, Sylvia. It was a marriage of convenience for both, and she endured his abusive hand for the security the other hand provided her.

One day she set a drink in front of a customer at the bar, and he asked her how she was. She was taken aback. It was a simple question, to be sure, but one she hadn't been asked in years. He listened to her and told her she would be successful. He asked what her dreams were.

One day the man said he could help her find a better job in Germany. She would make more money and be able to support her daughter by herself. She told him that her husband would never let her leave, but the man was confident he could work things out. She watched nervously as her husband and the man whispered by the bar, so excited by the thought of her potential freedom that she failed to notice the easy familiarity between the two.

Her husband nodded in approval; Elise would go to Germany. Sylvia would stay behind with her stepfather only until Elise had secured a job and found a school for her. Elise packed her bags and endured an exhausting road trip with two other girls who were also on their way to a better life. At one point the man awakened them. They were at a border crossing, and he needed their passports, he explained. They sleepily handed them over and immediately closed their eyes again.

When Elise opened her eyes again, she learned she was in the Netherlands. It was just for a visit, the man said, and it would be a shame to miss this popular tourist attraction along the way. Following instructions, Elise left the car with a man she did not know. She passed by window after window, a woman standing behind each one. The man had an unsettling smile. He led her through narrow cobblestone streets and eventually through the door of a brothel. They climbed three sets of stairs as Elise's wariness turned to fear and then dread. She was pushed into a room and read her rights, which were none. She was handed a bill of transport, a bill for the underwear and shoes laid out on the bare mattress, a bill for the bouncer who would lead men to her window, and a bill for the driver who would take her back and forth between this, her office, and an apartment she could not freely leave. She had left home to work independently and support herself and her daughter, and yet, hours later, her debt surpassed 10,000 euros.

She shook her head no. She flung the receipts at the man. He smiled. *Really?* He taunted. They had her passport. They knew where her daughter was. They *owned* her.

In the end she discovered no other option than to pay off her debt and buy her way to freedom. She needed her daughter back. And so she worked. Night after night, she endured the violation, the physical violence, and the horrendous physical damage to her body. In constant pain, she didn't bother to take medication because she hated her own body and welcomed the punishment. The world around her was incidental. She lived in a season of perpetual winter.

Eventually, Elise managed to find Sylvia, at the cost of a greater debt to her landlords. It was her daughter who allowed her to survive. She was a mother by day, helping her with home-work and nursing fevers and childlike worries. At night, she transformed her face with makeup and red lipstick, slid into a hated persona, and worked as a prostitute.

Days became months, and months, years. One day, she looked up without interest to respond to a tap on her window. A taxi driver smiled back at her. He had been there before, each time to bring a regular customer to the brothel. But this time he stopped to speak to Elise.

"Can I drive you home today?" he asked.

"I'm not sleeping with you. And I don't have any money for a taxi," she angrily retorted.

"I just asked if I could drive you home," he said.

She was taken aback, but she was too tired to argue. "OK, you can drive me home when my shift is over."

He smiled and patiently waited until she was ready. As he had promised, he took her home and waved good night as she walked to her door.

The next night, he returned, waiting until her shift ended. "Can I drive you home today?" he asked.

Night after night, he waited to drive her home. She grew accustomed to this, and in time he no longer had to ask. Instead, when the clock struck relief and she was able to leave, she quickly gathered her belongings, flipped off the red light, and walked outside to look for the one she knew was there waiting for her.

Slowly, slowly, she began to ease into his company. He helped her daughter with her homework. He took care of both of them. He wanted her to leave prostitution. He did not want to share her; he did not want her hurt and abused. But she was afraid and told him they would never let her leave. The taxi driver, himself a former criminal, called in a favor. He and some friends from low places visited Elise's pimp. He returned with her passport and her freedom.

She was free, but she was not free. Each night she hyperventilated, drenched in sweat and terrorized by the memories that imprisoned her within her own mind. Her health continued to decline. She was losing an inner battle.

One day, as she waited in the schoolyard to pick up her daughter, another mother walked up to her. This woman had tried to speak to her before, but Elise had shunned any human interaction. This woman was undeterred, and Elise learned that she, too, had worked in the red-light district. She told Elise about an organization that helped women like her. "You won't be able to get through this alone," she said. "They are safe. Let them help you."

And so Elise rang the bell one day. Before she could change her mind, the gate opened, and a young girl welcomed her inside. She was guided to a sofa and given a mug of hot tea. She talked. She cried. They helped her apply to school. They helped her travel to the Czech Republic so she could obtain proper papers. They saw her as human; they treated her with respect. They didn't ask for anything in return. There were no strings attached, no debts to pay, no coerced conversions to claim. But they spoke of a gracious and loving God, and for the first time, Elise wondered if he might actually exist.

Elise began to work through the agony that had begun long before she stood behind a window. She married the taxi driver, who brought her home for good. While it was true he could never claim that her body had been his alone, he felt no less rich. He alone had been granted permission to behold her soul and her future.

With the mercy brought about by the passing of time, a foundation of bitterness began to crack. Not completely; to say it disappeared and gave way to tender trust would be dishonest. But Elise was learning to love and to be loved. She went to school and earned a degree in psychology so she could help other women like her. She struggled to understand God, and he allowed her to fight. She wanted answers for everything that had happened. She kicked and struggled and raged, and he remained.

When Elise was diagnosed with leukemia, she fought to save the body she had once hated. She had not found all of the answers. She still wrestled to understand a God she believed was there, but one she desperately struggled to understand. Perhaps Elise understood more than she realized. Approaching death, she found rest from a life that had been fraught with pain. She looked back on her childhood, hurting and alone, being told she would never amount to anything. She was used and discarded, treated as less than human. But she was leaving this world as a woman who had loved and had been loved in return. She was leaving it as a mother, as a wife, as a friend, as a companion, as a teacher.

She was a person of consequence. She had not given up. She had fought to uncover the meaning of beauty in life, faithfulness to another, and faith in something greater than herself.

Elise's story was recorded to help other women in prostitution. Shortly before she died, the only thing that remained incomplete was the title. For this, she had an answer.

"Call it *Hope*," she said.

"I often had very little hope. I know what it feels like to be without hope. I need people who hope for me when I am losing hope myself. I live in hope. May my story bring you hope."[*]

⌣

I don't remember when the concept of *hope* was first explained to me. I don't remember the defining moment when I could identify or understand its longing. I know it did not happen when I was young, because to know hope is to understand the absence of something desired. I was provided for and safe and loved; I was not hungry or cold at night or sickly.

When I started college, I had to adjust to new routines and new friendships, and I needed to develop a sense of self that would shape my future. I had not visited my college before making the decision to attend, and apprehension began to set in when I arrived with my parents for orientation. They stayed a couple of days through student/parent seminars, and all too soon it was time for them to leave. I remember my failed attempt to keep the tears from brimming, and I actually sobbed, the kind where your stomach convulses, as my parents got into the car to drive away. I had always been a homebody, the kid who called her mother at two in the morning to pick her up from the slumber party.

---

[*] My thanks to Scarlet Cord — the Amsterdam-based ministry that provides alternatives for people in prostitution — for supplying the details of Elise's story.

I soon met a few friendly girls in my hall and learned my way around campus, but I quickly realized I did not quite fit in. As students compared the SAT scores that had gained them entry, I had hoped for the remote possibility that my home state of Georgia scored the test on a different scale. It was a good school with a respectably high emphasis on academics, so the student body was made up of valedictorians, AP students, and accomplished athletes. I was none of these things, and my free-spirited type B personality was outside of its element. I tended to the end of the spectrum that exercised the minimum amount of effort needed to achieve a grade I could live with. To this day I marvel when anyone receives an award for perfect attendance. It never occurred to me to even desire such an accolade. But when I arrived at the campus that would influence and define much of my self-perceptions, the standards of excellence and competition to be the best were applied to academics and life itself in ways I had not previously encountered.

During my first week, I stood at the single desk in my oddly shaped dorm room. The room was long and narrow, and at night we had to pull out the twin beds from each wall. In the morning, we had to push the beds back into the wall to create a narrow pathway to navigate through the room.

I was in a phase of loud animal prints that thankfully waned soon after freshman year. Leopard-printed throw pillows decorated the bed (when it was pulled out), and a matching black and gold rug lay across the length of the room. The print was too large for the micro space, but it gave a soft and warm buffer to our bare feet against the cold, gray tile floor that was likely once a stark white.

When I was in high school, it never occurred to me to worry about my body shape. Standing in a pair of shorts and a T-shirt,

I leveraged a foot against the single chair in the room and pulled on each tennis shoe, wrapping the laces into a bow. I had left the door of the room open and welcomed the hum of voices in the hallway. One girl poked her head in to say hello. She was very pretty, with blonde hair and blue eyes. I still remember her face, her name, and the city she was from. I'm not sure she remembered my name, even at the time, but she chatted for a minute and then pointed to my legs and said, "You know, you should really work on those thighs."

I was shocked and embarrassed. I looked down shamefully at the thighs I instantly hated, though I had never thought enough about them before to feel either criticism or satisfaction. I know I worked out that day, and the next, and I think just about every single day of college. I did have my share of late-night pizza, but I counted every calorie and fat gram, just like my friends did. Though we never discussed it, we had each calculated exactly how many meals we needed to deprive ourselves of so we could have two pieces of Papa John's pizza. And then we would work out afterward for a ridiculous amount of time. When one chose to have a salad, it was "hold the cheese, croutons, dressing, and sunflower seeds" — and everybody else quietly picked off anything from their plate that may have carried a calorie or ounce of flavor. In truth, we should have rallied around each other and helped each other. But we were all fighting our own battles of insecurity and contagious behavior, which only served to add to the plight each one carried.

In time, a defining moment came about through a dating relationship. I went to a Christian college, which meant there was no such thing as "casual dating." From the day you arrive on campus, dating is about future potential and ensuring that the necessary steps for the packaged life are put in place to follow the expected timeline. The order is: dating, graduation, marriage, babies, perfection. Each is to flow seamlessly into the next. Graduation is the wild card that can occur at any point on the timeline, and two weeks counts as "dating." Other than that, the formula is decidedly inflexible.

A boyfriend and I had shared ramen noodles, movies, and a family dinner or two, but one day the relationship took an unexpected dive from simple into intense. After dinner, without segue, he confessed to a severe addiction to hard-core pornography. It had been going on since he was a child, he explained.

I felt betrayed. Was I supposed to look like those girls? Is that what guys wanted? I wasn't built that way. Neither were the girls themselves. I had never read about pornography, heard it discussed, or known enough to know I should worry about it. I hated my thighs more; bought padded bras; wished I was taller, buffer, blonder, skinnier; and wondered if I could ever be pretty enough to keep a guy from choosing the image.

I went to talk to one of the trained counselors at school. Tears spilled down my face as I struggled to understand what this said to me, what it said about me. She shrugged her shoulders and said somewhat sympathetically, "This is something guys do."

Dissatisfied with this answer and determined to overpower it, I worked out like a maniac to try to improve something, anything, and everything. I spent hours climbing mechanical steps that led to nowhere. I took what is intended to be healthy and breathe life into my body and manipulated it to make it do exactly the opposite. In twisted perspective, I was not concerned if I harmed the body that faithfully cared for my heart. I wasn't deterred when my impulses growled to tell me my stomach was empty or when I struggled to think clearly because I was painfully hungry. By winter I had dropped sixteen pounds from my five feet three inch frame and weighed ninety-two pounds.

The relationship ended, but over time, in more than a few different dating relationships, the significant other confessed a problem with pornography. As it became an all-too-familiar conversation, my self-confidence declined from troubled to nonexistent, and I wondered if every girl faced this, or if it had something to do with me. I witnessed everything from the inner turmoil of one guy to complete indifference in another. "You're going to have to deal with it," he unapologetically told me.

I didn't know if it really *was* just my problem to deal with, and that was frightening because I *couldn't* deal with it and it was ravaging my sense of security and self-acceptance. To me, an image that reduced a three-dimensional being to the margins of a page had won, and I had lost. I read countless books and articles about every man's battle and tried to decipher confusing descriptions of a struggle that seemed to almost enable its beholders.

In retrospect, it would have been good for pornography to be discussed. Not just as a caution and support for the boys, but for the girls too. It is a pivotal stage in development when girls are seeking an identity and learning how to define themselves. Detrimental input without a voice for context and perspective can be devastating to a healthy development of a sense of self. In all the research I did, there was a glaring void about what a pornography addiction meant for "the other" in a relationship.

While studying phenomenology, a philosophical system founded by Edmund Husserl in response to relativism, University of Melbourne PhD candidate Damian Byers wrote a thought-provoking article ("Pornography and Damage") about what is harmful about pornography. I do not know Byers's spiritual worldview, as he makes no mention of it in the article. But it is a philosophical perspective that intelligently articulates pornography's casualties to the viewer and to the object, as he calls them. He sees pornography as the possibility of relation without the attitude of care. In truth, it is a victimless act that treats the viewer, the object, and the "significant other" with a carelessness that leaves every person with a battle to overcome.

I soon concluded that I could never be "enough," and I felt betrayed, not just by boyfriends, but also by the women themselves. Their presence kept touching a raw nerve within me that represented failure on my part. I began to view women whose bodies were marketed for sale as some kind of personal attack against me, a shameful reminder of the enough I could never be.

Until I met some of them. And I saw them as human. From the first conversation behind the window of a brothel, any unease I felt was dispelled. If we were to meet in a different context, we might have arranged to meet at Starbucks for a pumpkin spice latte. They were honest, smart, and easy to talk to. They were tired. They had resigned themselves to something that was not what they had dreamed of a lifetime ago. Their humanity was painted on their faces and on their story.

Most important, I realized that none of their decisions were some sort of personal attack against me. Their lives were much bigger than that. The reality was that they were trying to survive too — the things that had happened to them and their own decisions as well. Just like the rest of us. We have these moments in life when we realize those things that are the same in all of us, in spite of drastically different circumstances. So often, it seems, it has to do with the same needs and the same fears.

My sister called me recently and recounted the details of her morning. She had attended an event where a Jesuit priest told stories from his ministry, which is focused on helping former gang members reintegrate into society.

In one particular story, one of the young men came up to the priest as they traveled on a train and said he had just made a woman cry. "Is that OK?" he wondered. The priest said, "Well, that depends on why you made her cry." The boy said he was just standing next to her in line for the restroom, and he told her they were on this trip to tell their stories to people. So then when she heard his story, his audience of one started to cry.

The priest had smiled and assured him that it was OK. "She was crying because she sees in you exactly what I see in you today." Tears welled up in my sister's eyes, and as she glanced around the room filled with men and women in business suits, everyone seemed to be wiping their eyes. Why was that? It is unlikely that many people there had experienced life as a gang member and could relate to that aspect of the story.

It's the same reason I cried when I heard Annie's story. We do not have the same details to our lives, and some lives contain horrors we cannot fathom. But there is something in the human spirit — the desire to matter, to be seen, to have someone believe in us — that resonates in each one of us. When we see it clearly, when we *feel* it deeply, suddenly we're all the same. We're all on the same side of the window.

wild tresses

I was born early and with much drama — which seemed to be a foreshadowing of life to come. The drama that is, not the attentiveness to punctuality. There was no time to give my mother medication; there was barely time to make it to the hospital. She tells me that when I was born, my jet-black hair lay in soft curls around an evenly shaped head and earned an *awww* in unison from the nurses. And then they washed it. Apparently a mistake, for it awakened the beast within. In all of my baby pictures, I have a mass of defiant hair that protruded with a vengeance at various conflicting angles. I struggle to tame it to this day, but pretty hair in soft waves that lay as it should would have just been an anomaly to the rest of me.

I grew up in a Christian family. My father graduated from Trinity Evangelical Divinity School in Deerfield, Illinois, and was an itinerant evangelist in Niagara Falls, Canada, at the time I was born. Before this, he was a banqueting manager at a classy hotel in Toronto, having obtained a degree in hotel management from Delhi University in his home country of India. At the age of twenty, he left a familiar city with his older brother and ventured to a country completely unknown. His family followed them to Toronto two years later, after the certainty of knowing the oldest sons were successfully able to start a life in this new home.

My mother, a blonde-haired, blue-eyed beauty, quickly fell for the tall and lanky young chef from India who knew at that time how to mix a Bloody Mary for a hotel guest — ample fodder for not-so-quiet whispers and gossip in a conservative time. (He has long since forgotten how to handle a shaker.)

My mother is quiet and shy, at least at first glance. But thus began the tale of a life she has lived that shows her to be much more than meets the eye that only takes a first glance. She is a woman with spunk, who left her home and family and traveled around the world for fifteen months while her husband preached and she cradled a two-year-old on her hip with another baby on the way. She didn't know if her bed would be in a low-budget hostel or a missionary guest room on any given night, if the toilet would be more than a hole in the ground, or what body part of an animal might be served up as a delicacy for dinner.

Throughout my growing-up years, I never once heard her complain during what were certainly lonely nights with her husband miles away as she stayed up with an alarmingly feverish child or opened a box of macaroni and cheese for a wedding anniversary dinner for one.

In one of my all-time favorite books, *To Kill a Mockingbird*, the narrator is an eight-year-old firecracker named Scout. "I was born good but had grown progressively worse every year," she said to begin a chapter. I chuckle at her sentiments and echo her facetious confession. But if I said this to my mother, she would frown in sincere objection because she has refused to land there. Instead, she has always chosen to see the potential for a rainbow in my life, and I think she will paint it on the ceiling herself if she has to.

In her book *Goddesses in Everywoman*, Jean Shinoda Bolen discusses the century-old fascination we have for the fantastical stories from Greek mythology. A significant part of Greek literature and religion, mythology was the poetry that sought to explain the origin of the world and its spiritual realms, its heroes and heroines, and the moral dilemmas that resulted in catastrophic events. Centuries later, students still scrutinize the poetic accounts, perhaps most famously the *Iliad* and the *Odyssey*, attributed to Homer. Metered verse depicts the birth of Eros from Chaos and unveils images ranging from the intoxicating beauty of Aphrodite to those nothing short of disturbing when gods consume their own children out of jealousy.

Yet the myths have survived the test of time, and we find them relevant to our time and culture. The reason, Bolen suggests, is because of the way the characters mirror our human experience. While the myths are extraordinary, the elements of our nature are oddly familiar. The posed archetypes found in mythological characters are intriguing as we recognize traits of our humanity, of who we are and who we wish we were.

Bolen says that each woman differs from another, depending on which "goddess" archetype is prominent in her person.[3] These are not deities but essentially personality types that are far more revealing than whether or not you are a "lion" or a "golden retriever." For example, one woman values the traditional roles set before her and feels satisfied in the fulfillment of marriage and motherhood. Another finds satisfaction in her independence and the ability to achieve goals she has set forth for herself. Still another longs for solitude because it is in the moments of aloneness, as astutely distinguished from *loneliness*, that she finds a sense of home for herself. These individual traits are not exclusive or all-encompassing but in theory reveal a prominent set of hopes and ideals based on a corresponding leading character and her ideals.

The more complicated the woman, Bolen says, the more likely that there are many archetypes represented within her God-given personality. So what speaks to one part of her may say nothing to another equally present and important facet of her personality. This is why a woman with a fiercely independent streak may also feel a longing for companionship and possess a need for both respect and affirmation. It is not a contradiction within her but a testimony to her intricate layers.

I am an Artemis woman. Not exclusively, but she has an undeniable prominence in my life. Artemis feels strongly about her principles and is always on a campaign to right some perceived wrong on behalf of someone she thinks is misunderstood or overlooked. From the time she is contained by the rungs of a crib, she has a yearning for exploration and discovery. She does not want to be hemmed in; she does not toe the line for the sake of anyone's comfort. When she grows up, she is not inclined to settle in one place, for there is too much to see. But as Tolkien stated, "Not all those who wander are lost."[4]

She might run miles each day just to feel the wind against her face and to feel the strength and agility of the legs that carry her. She might campaign for political office. She is nontraditional, and stereotyped roles go against her nature. Aspirations and a hard head can lead to misguided perceptions that she is decidedly "unfeminine."

It is her intellect that she wants you to pursue, and a match of this kind she may seek in a man and mate. He will have to win an argument based on content and merit, not because of a superior gender. It is Artemis who represents the ideals of the women's movement, the equality and respect, a concern for the voiceless and the victimized. And before we discard the movement in its entirety for some of its misguided personifications, we should recognize that it is this voice that advocated for voting rights for women and safe childbirth and midwifery and initiated debate about what is exploited through pornography.

Artemis pursues her own course and appears strong and even defiant. Outwardly. But inwardly, as the saying goes, "No man [or, I would howl, woman] is an island." She maintains outward composure, seemingly unaffected by criticism from the key voices in her life. But internally she is profoundly wounded, and these voices in her head become her greatest obstacle, her supremely powerful enemy that may lead her, in the end, to transform into what they expect her to be. A significant relationship for the Artemis woman, and notably for every female archetype, is "Zeus," the father figure in her life. For Artemis, Zeus's perception of her will define her perception of herself. His voice of approval enables her to realize her full potential and provides grounding and confidence for who she is, thus preventing her spirit from being fatally wounded.

I had the opportunity to observe this recently as I sat, deep in conversation, with a good friend. She is beautiful, not the contrived kind of beauty, but the kind that just is. She has gentle eyes and long brown hair that falls in soft, natural curls. She recounted high school memories, and how difficult it was when boys did not ask her out on dates. "It hurt; it definitely did," she said, specific instances apparent on her face. "But it was really OK, because I knew my dad thought I was beautiful and smart and funny, and so I knew those boys were just stupid," she concluded with a shrug of her shoulders. Her husband, who knows that she is beautiful, who sees her mind equipped for unceasing meaningful conversation, who proudly brags about her latest artistic achievement, and who would rather spend an entire day with her than with anybody else, walked next to her.

The Artemis in each of us seeks to explore life, to extract every bit of nectar from it that we can. It is not a road to be traveled alone, for even a Miss Independent Greek Goddess needed the reassuring voice of another to help her find her own. Yet life is filled with a clamor of voices that speak to perceived gender roles, societal norms, and our own unrealized dreams. How do we drown out the chaos to hang on to a voice that is true, that reminds us of who we are when we forget, that compels us to realize our full potential and to embrace the divinely ordained adventure that is ours to live? And even if we could believe in such a thing, how do we see past our own fears and wounds to pursue it?

Some of us have wild tresses; others have silken strands like finespun gold. Some women will be wives; some will be mothers; others will walk an independent path in life. Their contexts are different, but they share dreams, and each plays the leading role in the adventure that is hers, rather than being simply swooped up in an adventure that belongs to someone else.

This is important because it influences how we approach living. Whether part of a shared adventure found in relationship or one lived out in the independent spirit of singleness, every woman has an equal role of importance in the opportunity and shared responsibility of a life course specifically given to her. No person is called to play second fiddle to another, for every life is called to an individual purpose. In his essay titled "Dreams at Sunset," F. W. Boreham writes, "Jesus ever kept His divine eyes wide open for any opportunity of preaching to the best of all congregations, a congregation of one."[5] This is not to minimize the gift of partnership, but we live in a culture that can oftentimes leave the one who is single feeling diminished or very small. Boreham's quote speaks of the heart of Christ and of a life affirming that every individual is seen and possesses an overflowing cup of eternal value.

The responsibility of each woman is to find the particularity of her calling, so to speak. It may be in concert with the calling of another; it may be a solitary path. But within each picture remains responsibility and opportunity of individual and epic proportion, and there is an individual triumph in distinctiveness when each woman finds the place where her own identity is secured. In this way, every life is ultimately an individual adventure of finding her place in God's plan. To surrender that is to surrender who you are.

deep recesses of longing

The body that carries me — the one I put through a bit of care-less torture — grants me a history and my heritage, reminders of where I have come from and of who came before me.

My paternal grandmother's name was Isabella. A special edu-cation teacher, she stood proudly at four feet ten inches tall and possessed a compassionate heart greatly out of proportion to any small stature. My parents tell me stories about her intellect, her wit, her spunk. They smile and tell me I would have loved her. They tell me she would have loved me too. My mother says Isabella used to get a twinkle in her eye and pinch her fingers just shy of together, the way you would grasp a dash of salt, to describe someone with a certain kind of fire. They were like a little chili pepper, she would say — so small, but they packed an awful lot of punch. I am told it was a description that fit her as well, and so perhaps this is why she had the twinkle and affection for another such pepper. I have also been told, many times and often in exasperation, that her eyes would have sparkled at me.

Sadly, I never had the privilege of knowing Isabella, as she died five years before I was born. I often wonder if she would have understood me and helped me to understand myself. She gave me not just her petite height and possibly those very thighs another dared to critique, but perhaps some of her spirit as well. She connects me to a place I only first visited at the age of sixteen but have returned to countless times since. It is a place that is the enviable setting for stories — and not just my own.

⁓

Born in India in the 1800s, Rudyard Kipling chose India as the setting for his compilation of tales known as *The Jungle Book*. He wrote adventurous stories of lions and tigers and bears, of assumed danger and escape, both literal and metaphorical. The most famous of his characters was Mowgli, the "man cub" raised by wolves in the Indian jungle. Kipling is said to have filled the tales with all he "heard of or dreamed about the Indian jungle." I easily understand why Kipling chose this for his setting of wonder-filled tales of adventure. India is magical.

You must leave your need for personal space behind, for at any given moment, whether enclosed in a taxicab or exposed on the street, you will be surrounded by men, women, children, auto-rickshaws, taxis, exhaust fumes, carts, scooters, goats, cows, and the smells of samosas, jasmine, spices, manure, and trash warmed by the blazing sun. It will fill and enhance your senses. It is a portrait of life at work with apparent beauty and glaring tragedy, and it asks you to look on it all.

The heart of India is its people, and it is a heart like no other. It is rich, not from what it owns, but from what it will offer to you, even while you are still a stranger. It will take you in, bring you into its own, cook a feast for you, provide a bed to rest, ask about your family, say that you are pretty, or ask why you have put on weight. It will take you through markets of fine silks and hand-stitched saris. It will show you dancing, jingling anklets and toe rings, and vibrant colors of red and pink and green and marigold because it likes to decorate and make things beautiful.

It will take you through its cities, where street numbers were assigned as a building was completed and not by consecutive order. It will take you to the magnificent Taj Mahal, which was commissioned by a grieving widower as a tomb for the wife he lost in childbirth. It will tell you that he died imprisoned in a tower by his son, and that a single window provided him with one simple view — that of the Taj Mahal.

It will show you strands of pearls in Hyderabad, pink stone in Jaipur, beautiful white sand beaches in Goa. It will introduce you to basmati rice and curries that have been simmering for hours, pistachio ice cream, and fried doughnuts floating in sweet syrup, and it will teach you how to eat with the fingers of your right hand. It will show you how to slap dough into chapatis. It will fold its hands to say *namaste* as you pass by the elderly woman on the side of the road. It will impress you with its propensity for academic excellence in technology, engineering, and medicine. It taps on your car window, the beautiful face of a little girl with round dark eyes and black eyelashes, clasping her fingers together and drawing them to her mouth to tell you she needs food.

India will introduce you to graciousness, where the opportunity to serve is held in high regard. It will show you where Mother Teresa left her heart, in the city where men still pull the weight of a rickshaw on foot. It will take you by hand down narrow dusty streets, past colored buildings where paint is chipping off, bars line the windows, and dark eyes stare out from inside.

It works hard for a living; it remembers you when years have passed since it last saw you, as it affectionately calls out *baba* or *baby, little boy* or *little girl*. It will sing passionately for you; it will hold up traffic and flail its arms to another driver whose arms flail with equal passion; it will walk down the street holding hands with its brother. It values symbolism and tradition. It wiggles its head and tells you "no problem" to whatever you ask. It will redefine dedication and honor, family and religion. It will punish failure, and around the next corner, it is a picture of long-suffering in faith past poverty, past unanswered prayers, past a life that has been hard.

You will feel special, amazed, full, stirred, naive, helpless, enraged, awakened — and all in the first day. India is magical.

———

I stood next to my summer intern, hovering over the belt in baggage claim, looking at her with a mixture of probable doubt and hope afloat. Luggage had been passing us by for the better part of an hour, but none of the red, green, or black suitcases, boxes wrapped with multiple rounds of tape and string, identifying strands of ribbon tied around handles, or shrink-wrapped some-things were ours.

I had almost given up and was internally reprimanding myself for having checked luggage and put my faith in the system again. Having lost clothing, gifts, and multiple treasured flatirons in luggage that takes that one-way trip, I now try to avoid checking anything in. This means my carry-on often feels like it exceeds even my own body weight. On a recent trip where I had been en route to somewhere I can't remember for close to thirty hours, I was exhausted and had not slept, showered, or eaten in too long a time to be healthy for myself or anyone in close proximity. I boarded another flight, and as I went to lift my backpack into the overhead one more time, my right arm shook in final protest, and the bag fell back down. I could not lift it up. I don't like asking for help, but I returned the looks of fellow passengers in the surrounding seats, responsibly belted in and calmly watching my struggle. I could only pause to engage my arm in exaggerated calisthenics to keep from blurting out, "Really? I mean *really*?"

But this time, against my better judgment, I had checked in the suitcase that I now longed to see. I was going to be gone for three weeks, and it held clean clothes, shampoo, and granola bars. As a stretch of empty belt passed us by, we stayed firmly rooted, not wanting to give up. And then, we glimpsed the neglected bags dropping onto the belt. We dragged them off and pulled them behind us as we walked out the double doors and into Mumbai. Even though it was the middle of the night, the summertime heat enveloped us as we stepped out to greet it. Within moments I felt sticky, as waves of heat seemed to radiate from my body. But it has become a welcome feeling, a reminder of a place I love and that is part of my story.

We checked into our hotel and ordered rice and *dhal* to be brought to our room, even though it was just hours before dawn. My intern, Emily, said she felt bad staying in this lovely hotel, knowing that people were lying on the street outside our secured doors. I appreciated her perspective and explained that we were just here for a single night. I genuinely liked her father when I met him and answered his stern but endearing questions about arrangements for his daughter for the summer. He had a good sense of humor. He also happened to be a Jewish attorney from Philly who was temporarily entrusting the totality of his daughter's well-being to my management. I began praying for her safe return — and thus my continuing existence — before she even left. It is difficult to find the in-between in India, and given our nocturnal arrival, safety was the priority. The plan was to transfer the next day to the place that would become her home for one month. This profession creates many different worlds within your own, from the chandeliers of a nice hotel to the floor of a hut on an only slightly inhabited island.

And so we enjoyed the hot water and crisp linens for the short night and checked out in the morning. We started the day by going into Kamathipura, the red-light district in Mumbai. We visited a children's shelter that began as a night care center for the children of women working in the brothels. Before the shelter, the children were in the rooms when clients arrived, sometimes drugged to limit their awareness of what was transpiring.

We walked into clinics that provided free dentistry, medical care, and HIV treatment for women in the district. I folded my hands to greet friendly faces that have become familiar and met the warm embrace of Sunita, the coordinator of an outreach team that finds women in need of treatment who are too sick to walk to the clinic. She herself once worked in a brothel and then became a brothel madam. Today she remains in Kamathipura, a place that brought her so much pain, to help bring freedom to girls who remind her of herself once upon a time.

Emily and I traveled outside of the city, where the crowded street became an unpaved road leading to a home for children who had been brought out of the brothels and off the streets. A boy with the cutest grin in the world greeted us, his dark brown eyes sparkling as his bare little feet pattered to the door.

We continued on to a home for older children who had been living on the street in drug addiction. They were now in school, and we sat in on a music lesson as they learned to strum electric guitars and write music of their own. We met girls who had been sold and victimized and now walked the flower-lined pathways of a home that was entirely theirs — a place where they were safe.

The day had been full, and I could see Emily's eyes beginning to glaze over. She had graduated from a university in California one month before joining our team for two months. She would spend it overseas, conducting research and project evaluation on our behalf for initiatives that had received financial grants during the year and other initiatives we were considering for future grants. The endeavor was significant, and she bravely accepted the responsibility.

I was very fond of Emily, and she was right for this job, not only because of her intelligence and teachable spirit, but also because she had a discernment that cannot be taught and a heart that cannot be crafted through employee orientation. She didn't just look; she *felt* on the inside that which her eyes could only see.

At the end of the first day, I walked into the room and found her curled up in the fetal position on one of the twin beds. Pathways of tears streaked her face, and seeing a familiar face invoked a new hydraulic surge. Technically I was her boss, but I was also her friend. A maternal instinct seemed to kick in, and my heart just ached for her.

We skipped dinner that night. She cried tears for the little one with HIV, for the girl who had been locked in a room and raped repeatedly for eight years, for the boy who fled a home of abuse and ended up in drug addiction on the street. "I read the statistics, I researched the issues. I thought I knew them. I thought I was ready for it. But there is no way to ever be ready for it," she said between sobs. "Does it get easier?"

"I don't think it gets easier. You always feel it just as deeply," I answered, "but you learn to cope." And I truly believed those words at the time.

The next morning, I fought back the tears that threatened to fall as I said good-bye to her. I was leaving her there to do her job, and I was continuing on to do mine. We would meet at home in six weeks. I could see her own eyes glistening, and I hugged her tightly, whispered something silly to try to keep my emotions together, hiked up my long, purple peasant skirt to allow the new henna tattoo to dry, and jumped into the Jeep to make the long drive back to Mumbai and eventually the airport.

I was taking a detour to visit a children's home, a home that organized international adoptions. I was accompanied by our ministry partner, Devaraj, who directs the program that Emily was visiting. After several years of working together, his family has become more than just partners in ministry. We drove up and down the same street, trying to find the address in a maze of buildings that all looked alike and whose street numbers did not follow a pattern, or were nowhere to be found.

I sat in the back seat as Devaraj rolled down the window and asked a passerby for directions in Hindi. The exchange continued for some time as he pointed, nodded, and gestured. I thought we were making progress. When they were finished, Devaraj rolled up the window and said, "He doesn't know it." I smiled.

Eventually we pulled up to a concrete building, and he clucked with satisfaction. I didn't see a sign or a number on the outside, but he had found it and nodded to let me know I could get out of the car. We were here.

I sat in an informational meeting taking notes in my black moleskin notebook as I learned the specific and complicated details of international adoption in India. It was complicated, but not impossible. Before I left, the social worker asked, "Would you like to see some of the babies?" I nodded my head in certain affirmation.

I stepped into a room filled with white cribs. Three tiny

bundles lay nearby, cocooned in pink blankets. Their eyes were closed, and long black eyelashes lay still, completely undisturbed by a nearby cry. They had entered the world just the day before. My eyes filled with tears, and the social worker smiled kindly. I wished I could hold them. I wished I could keep them. Instead I could only wonder what life would hold for each of them. Would somebody take care of them and spend endless hours perfectly content just to watch their gorgeous eyelashes rest in sleep?

I slowly backed out of the room, wishing I were allowed to stay. Before we left, the social worker wanted to introduce my friend to a little boy. He was six years old, and he needed a placement. The boy's mother had abandoned him when he was small, and an international adoption had been interrupted. Knowing that Devaraj led an organization that included an outreach to children in Mumbai, she thought he might be of help in the future. She asked us to wait in the lobby while she brought the young boy to us.

I saw him coming from a distance, his bare feet shuffling against the floor as he held her hand and walked toward us. He wore jeans and a navy blue and green plaid button-down shirt that was untucked. His hair was a medium shade of brown, and his eyes a milk chocolate. He had a hearing aid in his left ear. As I bent down to shake the hand he extended, he shyly attempted to speak to me in the English he was still a bit uncertain in. I fell in love with him at that moment. If legalities had not stood in the way, I would have brought him home.

I walked outside and covered my face with my hands as tears spilled. I remembered the words I had said to Emily only a day before: "… you learn to cope." I shook my head at my own sentiments. For it seemed that around the next corner there was always something that would break my heart anew.

Months passed, and each day I thought of six-year-old RJ, as my sister called him. I wondered how he was doing, and for a while the children's home was patient with my regular messages to inquire about him. Legally, they could not give him to me. But Devaraj had been there too, and there *was* something he could do. In time they gave permanent custody to his children's home, and RJ had a family. And while I was confident he was safe and well cared for, I couldn't help but feel as though I had lost something. It didn't really make sense, because the feeling was that of losing something that I never actually had. I had experienced something special in a numberless building in Mumbai that day. It was the stirrings of love, sadness, hope, disappointment, and gratitude — a typical day in India.

Eight months later, I had the opportunity to see RJ again. He did not remember me, but I felt emotion I cannot articulate as I shook his little bronzed hand again and introduced myself to him as if it were the first time we met. He sat next to me and ate a bowl of pistachio ice cream. I smuggled a second one to him, and when he finished, he handed me his empty plastic bowl and ran off to play with his friends. I knew he was in a good place, but mostly I felt sadness.

A few weeks after I returned home, someone asked me if I had ever thought of adoption. I don't know if he expected my answer, but I said I had actually considered it. I told him that a friend in Mumbai had taken me to a child services center to discuss the possibility. I gave the abridged version of the story and concluded by saying that it didn't work out for me, but the center had given custody to my friend and his ministry. And I added that I had recently seen him, and he was doing well.

My questioner smiled sincerely and said, "That's a great story of how everything worked together and he now has a home. You must feel really happy about that." It's funny. I had not realized that it was a good story. I had only clearly been able to see what *I* had lost, and in my narrow perspective, I failed to recognize the greater gift there for me to unwrap. Evidently, I was not meant to be the one who would provide RJ a home. He doesn't remember me now, and when I see him again, I will likely shake his hand and introduce myself again to dark eyes that will reflect no recognition. But I don't think it will hurt as much the next time.

The next time I look at the tone of my skin, the shape of my hands, and the build of my legs, I want to see a story. One that reminds me of my grandmother Isabella, one that journeys to her roots in India, to my roots in India, a rich stage for a million little stories from a past that we share. I imagine she would have told me them all, in her thick accent, as she no doubt wiggled her head from side to side in typical Indian mannerism. I will always be connected to this past, and it continues to reveal to me my present. It beckoned me into a numberless building in Mumbai one day. And the story continued. It was not defined by the outcome, regardless of whether or not the other players were aware I was a character on its stage. It became part of my story the day I decided to participate in something and go after a dream that might be left unmet and leave a hope unrealized.

I've learned that longing is a little like shame. Both seem to be a difficult thing to shake, although for completely different reasons. But they find a common ground in setting up camp in the deep recesses of inside.

real faith

The earth had exploded into miniature sunbeams. I was not in India, but in a beautiful country of a different kind. I was well into my twenties and enjoying a memorable afternoon in an open sunflower field in South Carolina. A friend of mine had an aunt and uncle who owned a farm with acres of country hills and grand oak trees that could be the setting for the kind of novel that would carry me home to the South from wherever I read it. A group of us loaded into an old pickup truck and drove out to an open expanse of uninterrupted freshly cut green grass that filled the air with the smell of spring. Through the radio speakers, Waylon Jennings was crooning about unrequited love, prison, and his mama.

We jumped out of the pickup and pulled down the hatch to hop up onto the bed of the tailgate. Dangling my legs over the edge, I watched as my friend loaded shells into the breech of a shotgun and closed the action. He handed me ear protection, which I slipped over my head like headphones. The skeet traps launched, and we took turns hitting the clay targets. The experience was freeing and exhilarating. By the end of the afternoon I felt like a combination of Annie Oakley and Lara Croft.

Except for one mishap: the ear protection got in my way each time I moved the shotgun to my shoulder and lowered my eye to line up the beads on the barrel with the target. I asked my friend if I really needed those things on my ears. He said he had foam earplugs, but only one. Since I was a bit of a novice/fool, it seemed like a better idea to me, and I exchanged the ear protection gear for a single earplug. As the pellets traveled through the barrel of the shotgun and exploded into the air, I felt as if my eardrum had done the same thing. I clicked my jaw and rubbed my left ear, trying to assuage the piercing sound of ringing.

Several days later, I could still hear the incessant hum, the sound of the acoustical sensors of my inner ear, my stereo cilia, dying. I had learned this from my bargain-sale trivia textbook I knew would come in handy one day.

I had graduated from college five years earlier, but my senior year of college was like shooting skeet with one earplug.

There were so many well-intentioned inquiries:

- *Will you go for your master's? It's the new bachelor's ...*
- *Will you be doing "kingdom" work, or the other kind?*
- *It's not about higher education; it's about real-life experience.*
- *Are you getting married? How many children do you want? [The biological clock is ticking, you know.] Have you found a job?*

And then there were the roller coasters of my own ideas:

- *The Peace Corps has a posting in Mauritius ...*
- *I'd love to work in a downtown skyscraper, the kind you need a badge to get into.*
- *The Air Force is recruiting ...*
- *Can someone please explain what "nonkingdom" work is?*

In theory, in our early twenties we are supposed to decide these things for the rest of our lives. The problem is, many of us don't truly know anything about any of those things, or about ourselves for that matter. Honestly, the one saving grace is ignorance. I'm convinced this is the magic of the early twenties, a naiveté that actually serves a purpose in propelling us to risk, to aspire, to dream. It's what makes us really annoying, yet potentially successful.

We don't realize that a misfire can invoke incessant ringing. Instead, the misinformed belief that we are invincible compels us to try. The older we get, the more difficult it becomes to take a risk because we are then all too aware of our propensity to fail, that the stereo cilia can actually die, and they do not regenerate.

So armed with bliss my senior year, I couldn't wait to graduate. It was an exciting time of tunnel vision for potential. I interviewed in a few corporate offices, and while I awaited potential offers, the brilliant thought occurred to me that I would like to go overseas. To study Spanish. And work with children. And discover a new country. I found a place online, exchanged e-mails, and eventually confirmed that I would arrive in Central America after graduation. There is a chance this is the kind of thing that made my father prematurely gray.

I remember the time of fearlessness fondly. But in truth, the naiveté of younger years should not be confused with courage. It is only courage when we know the cost of failure. It is only faith when there is the potential for doubt. And it can only be won when we have to fight for it.

Jacoline was the oldest of two daughters born to her parents in Cape Town, South Africa. Her father died when she was six years old, and her mother struggled to raise her two girls alone. But she was an A student in school and had decided that she was going to be a teacher. She had ambitions and dreams, like every other girl her age.

Her mother remarried when she was thirteen years old. This difficult time of transition soon became a nightmare for the teenage girl when her stepfather sexually abused her. When he violated a boundary that was never to be crossed, he also dismantled the God-given boundaries inside of her, given to help her navigate away from harm. Her dreams and ambitions eroded away, and she left home. Living on the street, she began to use drugs. Soon she was working in prostitution in an effort to support herself.

"It's a very last resort," she says. "It's like being subjected to rape over and over again."

In ten years, she gave birth to two children, but each time they were taken away from her. Realistically, she knew she could not properly take care of them, as she didn't have a home. One day, one of her clients asked her to marry him. He loved her, he said. She thought this would mean she could leave the brothel. No more having to entertain clients; no more having to feel disgusted after they left. No more feeling lost, because she would belong to someone.

She married him, but none of the things she counted on came to be. He wanted her to continue working in the brothels. "We can use the extra money," he told her. This felt worse to her than it had before. For before, there was no one who was supposed to care, who was supposed to want to protect her. But now there was, and he wanted to share her with other men. Her body was a form of income for him, and she felt used and betrayed.

She had secretly wanted another child for some time, someone who would be hers to love and to take care of. When she saw women walking down the street pushing baby strollers, her heart would ache, and she wished so badly that she had one of her own. When she heard babies crying in a restaurant, she wasn't irritated, as many were. Instead, her eyes filled with tears as she wished that the cry belonged to a part of her and was hers to soothe and console. She thought often about the two children she had given birth to. They would be three and five. She wondered if they were happy, if they would ever ask about her, if they would ever forgive her.

She remembers the moment when she believed she was pregnant again. She felt a stirring in her spirit, and something told her that her body contained something that was filled with life. Soon afterward, the stirring was confirmed by a pregnancy test. She couldn't be certain if the baby was her husband's or a client's, though deep inside she believed she knew.

It didn't matter to her, because she was thrilled. This was her "third time lucky," as she called the baby who grew in her belly. This one would not be taken from her; this one would be hers to keep. She was walking, breathing, eating, and sleeping for someone other than herself, and she loved knowing that her body was working, not just to sustain life for her, but for a life that she helped to create, one completely dependent on her.

She had weeks of morning sickness at all times of the day, wishing it was called something different to better describe what she was experiencing. She tried to eat bland crackers and drink lots of water, like everyone told her to. She worried about the baby growing properly, and so she tried to eat fresh fruits and vegetables to keep him healthy. She was his mother, and it was her job to take care of him in every way she could. She knew that his body was connected to hers through an umbilical cord, that her very life sustained his, that her body kept him nourished, and that when her baby was hungry, she was hungry too.

After five months she felt him kick. At six months she saw the unmistakable print of a tiny fist pressed against her belly. She talked to him all the time, as she had heard he would know her voice before he ever squinted to look at her face for the first time. They had a bond that no one could break.

As her belly began to swell, so did her feet. She was exhausted, and her back ached, but she didn't care. She never complained, silently or aloud. And right on time, she felt the first pangs of labor. She was alone at the hospital, with no one to tell her to keep pushing or to cheer her on. Sweat dripped down her face, and her eyes were tightly shut. She struggled and cried out, remembering that after the labor, she would hold him in her arms. She then heard her son cry, and the world never sounded the same again. For thereafter it would always carry within it a melody, however sad a song.

When the baby was born, it was obvious from his appearance that it was not her husband's child. And with nothing left to keep them together, she and her husband divorced, and she was once again on her own. She had no way to support herself and soon turned to the one thing she knew. She arrived with her baby at the house. The woman in charge took one look at the bundle and rolled her eyes, but she waved them in. The young mother hit the streets each day and night to sell drugs. She was using again, too, to keep herself awake and alert. And while she worked, the woman in charge took care of her baby.

One day she bypassed her normal route and turned down a different street toward the waterfront. The man she believed to be the baby's biological father was there on his navy ship. He had been a regular client for a period of time. She thought that when she told him about his son, he would marry her and then she could be off the streets. But he didn't want to marry her. He wasn't angry; he wasn't happy. He wasn't anything at all except uninterested. He callously shooed her away, the way one gets rid of a pesky mosquito or an annoying dog.

She was devastated as she walked home with her head hung low, unsure of how she was going to provide for her child. When she got back, the door was locked. She banged on it persistently, and finally the woman cracked it open. She told her she was no longer welcome there, and she was keeping the baby. She had grown attached to him, and no one would give him back to his mother, a homeless drug addict. The distraught mother had nowhere to turn, no one to call. She sobbed and wailed, pleading for her baby. But the door would no longer be open to her.

She knew she was unhealthy and wasn't taking proper care of him. But she loved him. She wanted her son. She went back to a familiar street where she often worked, and week after week passed. She was lost and broken, having no idea how to find her way to a home or what that even was. There was nothing, and although she was trying to survive, she didn't know why.

She saw a familiar face one night, a woman with long blonde hair. She had come by often, talking about the Bible and Jesus and new life. It hadn't interested the forlorn woman, who believed God had forsaken her. She had heard about him growing up, but she had given up believing he was real a long time ago. But this time the woman named Helen spoke of wanting to open a home where girls could stay. She asked Helen to let her know when a room was ready, that she would like to be the first one there. Both stayed true to their word, and she was soon living in a house with a bed, in safety, with someone to help her overcome addiction and leave behind a lifestyle she no longer wanted.

In three years, she moved in and out eight times. Sometimes she was sure she was back on her feet and ready to leave. But without anything new to turn to, she would go back to selling drugs or her body — the only things she knew how to do, the one world she knew how to exist in. Sometimes she was focused on wanting to get her son back. Sometimes she turned back to drugs.

"It was the drugs more than anything that called me back. Every time I went back I used. And then I'd go back to prostitution. I had to use to be able to go back," she explained.

She had just moved in for the ninth time when I met her. She seemed real and sincere — a woman who had experienced hurt. We talked casually for a bit. I didn't ask her what brought her there, since I didn't feel I had earned the right to know any details. Instead, I asked her, "If you could do anything in the world, what would it be?"

Instantly, she replied, "I'd be a chef." She loved to cook and was always eager to switch chores with anyone who had kitchen duty for the day. It was a worthy dream — one that, it seemed, someone should be able to make happen. When I returned home, Wellspring began researching culinary schools in the area. We called a school and explained that we were interested in giving a scholarship to a potential student, and they explained the payment details.

We called Helen to tell her we were considering providing a scholarship to culinary school, but that our potential student would have to initiate and complete the standard application process. If she were accepted, we would provide the scholarship.

She did exactly that and began school at the start of the term. She began to send pictures of her classes — and even of the Moroccan dish she made for an assignment. And then came an e-mail humbly asking if she could bring her son home. She would need help with the expenses, with his education. But she knew where he was, and now that she was in a stable place, she believed she could get him back. The reply was a no-brainer and simple: Bring him home.

Eighteen months later, the boy graduated from first grade, and she graduated at the top of her class. She was offered a full-time position as a chef in the restaurant of a four-star hotel in Cape Town. That was two years ago, and she remains on their staff today.

I was in Cape Town last May on Mother's Day. I went with her son to have lunch at her restaurant. We sat at a table with a white tablecloth. As I turned around, I saw her. She was wearing her full chef uniform as she walked out of the kitchen with a huge grin on her face. I will never forget that beautiful moment. I'm not sure which one of us was more proud. She looked like she belonged — like she had been there all along.

She had written these words in a note to Wellspring a few weeks after she started school:

> I just finished watching a movie called *Seabiscuit* about a horse and a jockey that both faced really difficult circumstances. Both had little chance of success until they were spotted by the right people, who invested time into them. It is a wonderful, true story of how they overcame and became winners. Well, I really can identify with them. Thank you so much for believing in me, and I trust, with God's help, I am going to be a winner too. My son is here for the weekend, and he can't wait to be moving in and going to his new school. I pray that God will bless and prosper you and give you all the desires of your heart as He is with us … You have made a dream come true.

To this day, she affectionately signs all her notes as "Biscuit." The dream was hers, put in her heart by God. He spoke to someone, who brought her into a home. He spoke to us to help her get into school. She had been hurt, and she needed people who were able to see past the obvious to the breadth of potential , the glimpse at what could be. But the dream — now that is all hers. For it was birthed and realized because of something she carried inside of her all along.

chapter 7

shaping liberties

After her shift at the small hotel where she welcomed guests in reception, Bijal and I met outside. She had exchanged her burgundy suit for faded jeans and a black T-shirt. She flashed me a grin as we hopped onto her motorbike and weaved through traffic to get to Little India, even though we were actually in Malaysia. When we arrived at our destination, I threw my right leg over the back of the bike and pulled off my helmet. I could feel my eyes dancing. I loved the thrill of the wind against me as I leaned into it on a motorbike.

She laughed and told me not to tell my father we had been on her bike. I grinned and ran a hand through my tangled hair. We walked down the street as Hindi music blared through speakers outside a CD store, past rows of jeweled bangles and gold nose rings for sale. She pointed to the restaurant we had been to previously, and I nodded in agreement. The smell of curry filled the air, and we entered the small room with white walls and small tables.

I filled my aluminum cup with water from the cooler nearby, and servers brought us mutton curry and chicken *tikka* served on banana leaves. She asked if I wanted a fork. "Not if you're not using one," I answered. She grinned, and we buried our right hands in curry and rice. I ripped off a piece of warm *naan* and closed my eyes to savor the flavor of the fresh bread that had been retrieved from the nearby clay oven only moments before.

I asked about her four children, and she filled me in on school activities and birthdays, sicknesses, and report cards. I then asked about her husband, knowing it would take us into her angst.

I had known Bijal for three years, and her life has definitely not been easy. Her husband was abusive. A recent argument had resulted in a few bruises along her arms and a large bruise on her hip when a firm shove sent her falling to the unforgiving floor. He did not give her money to take care of the kids or pay for their education. She had a job — a good job by local standards — but it didn't pay nearly enough to cover all the bills. She did not have her own transportation to get to work, and so she spent two hours each way and much-needed Malaysian ringgit on public transportation. Wellspring had given her money to buy a scooter and was sending money each quarter to cover the education costs for her children as well as for some basic living needs.

I had been to see her each year, and the last time we met, she told me about her husband's mistress. Bijal has a spunky personality, full of energy and passion. When she is upset, it is expressed with equal passion. Anger had flared up in her eyes when she told me about her husband. When I asked about him now, she answered, "The other girl — she is pregnant." I raised my eyebrows and stopped eating to look at her carefully. I didn't say anything; I knew she had not finished talking.

Tears filled her eyes at one point, but it was not as much from sadness as deep anger. She was tired of being disrespected. She had chosen a "love" marriage rather than an arranged marriage. "How foolish," she said as she shook her head. "What is love?" she asked, without pausing for an answer. Another woman was going to have his baby. The mistress lived down the street, and it was all so humiliating. "Why do I have to put up with that?" she asked. She had gotten angry with him about it, and he responded to her words with physical violence. He had hit her across the face, leaving more bruises on her body.

"Why should I stay? I can leave, right?" she asked. This time she was waiting for an answer.

I exhaled in a loaded sigh. I knew the answer was far more complicated than I wanted it to be. She was being abused; she was being hurt. And I knew that these things tend to escalate. I wanted to tell her she didn't have to stay. Even in my own culture, issues of leaving a marriage are treacherous ground for any outsider, for we are entering into something that will affect a woman or man for the rest of their life, no matter which option they choose. It is easy to hand out advice when we are not the ones who have to live with the dire consequences. Even so, there are some issues that are more black-and-white than others.

But she didn't share my culture. She was from a Muslim background, and her options were drastically different.

"What about your children?" I asked.

She looked down at the table. Her husband would never let her take them with her. She would have to leave them behind.

"Where would you go?" I asked. "Where would it leave you?"

She could not go home as a divorced woman, she said. It was not an option to stay here; he would never allow her to do that. She would be on her own.

"How would you support yourself?" I asked. She shrugged her shoulders. "And the kids — what would happen to them?" I asked again quietly.

She didn't say anything. She just nodded her head. I felt sick to my stomach because I didn't know what to tell her. My country, my culture, allows me an option she doesn't have. We might face personal bias and judgment, but we have a viable option. Her life was not that simple. Leaving would have extreme consequences, surely for her children and likely for herself as well. She would be leaving behind her children and her family. She would have no job, no money, no support, and in addition to the obvious problems all this entailed, it would leave her susceptible to a vast array of new horrors.

But so would staying, and I was painfully aware of this. She would go back home tonight. She would endure his temper, his wrath, the strike of his hand. Not me. I would not be there. I would not be there to take the brunt of his fist, to put ice on a swollen eye, to take her to the hospital if she needed to go. I would not be there to hear the horrible things he said, to witness him bruising her on the inside to a detriment greater than outside marks could ever reveal. I would not be there if he struck a blow that was fatal one day.

I did not want to give her advice. Both options required a price and an enormous risk that I wasn't going to have to pay. She carried a burden I could not take from her, and I hated that reality. Even the discussion brought me a sense of doom, the recognition of something I had to live with that I didn't want to. I could ask questions, but I didn't know what to tell her to do. She was trapped, and her worldview was confined to the frame of her reality.

———

I was twenty-six years old and walking into a maximum-security prison. I was in Africa and visiting a friend who, together with her husband, had launched a prison ministry in Cape Town. Victoria is petite, with blonde hair and brown eyes, and looks like

Christy Brinkley. She was once a model in New York City, successful in her career and surrounded by people and an industry and community that sought to make her life comfortable. Now she lived with her American husband and three young children in a gated community in a city with one of the highest crime rates in the world. I believe both environments required strength of a different nature.

The prison guards knew her when we walked in the door, and they greeted her in a friendly manner. I signed a piece of paper that I think was probably absolving anyone of responsibility should anything unfortunate happen to me.

We walked down a long hallway and stopped outside a cell door. We paused to wait for the buzzing sound that would alert us that the door was open. We walked several paces down another colorless hallway and stopped at another cell door. Again, a buzzing sound. When we entered through a third door, we stood in a cell block that contained hundreds of female prisoners.

Some were guilty of crimes; others insisted on their innocence. Many were from foreign lands and said they had come to work as housekeepers — or so they believed. When they were ill-treated, they tried to run away. But they did not get far. Their employers pressed charges, accusing them of crimes, like stealing or even breach of contract. Without knowledge of a common language, they were unable to defend themselves. They were arrested and placed behind bars, the door loudly shutting behind them. A court date was set, and each woman's innocence or guilt would be determined at that time. When the court date arrived, a prison guard tapped on the cell door and called out a name. The woman would not know where she was going or what would happen when she got there. She would not understand anything they said, and no interpreter would be provided. She would be guided into a courtroom, where a judge behind an imposing bench would speak additional words she could not understand.

She would shuffle to the podium to stand before the one who would decide her fate. She would use the language she knew, because there was nothing else she could do. The judge would shake his head no; he could not understand what she was saying. She would become more and more desperate, feeling helpless to do what we do every day without thought — communicate. Her future depended on it. The judge would slam down the gavel, pound a stamp on a piece of paper, and dismiss her. She never really had a chance for freedom.

And thus each cell was filled to maximum capacity with despair, with anger, with hopelessness, with a desire for revenge. Some were guilty of committing crimes; others were victims of unfortunate circumstances or exploitation. Some of the stories of violence perpetrated on each other inside the cell were horrific. With a shortage of space and an overwhelmed justice system, these women would be there for years, just awaiting a trial.

There was a separate section reserved for women with children. If they were pregnant when they were arrested, they gave birth in prison. The child would remain for up to five years before the mother had to find a family member or friend to take custody.

I was trying to take it all in, trying to comprehend what this life was like. But in truth, I absolutely couldn't. I could feel sympathy, sorrow, anger, or fear on their behalf; but I had not experienced the poverty and the desperation to find food and to survive that may have led to theft, or the anger and sense of injustice that may have led to murder. I stood with them behind bars, but I had the power to determine when I was leaving. And they did not.

When it was time to leave, the buzzer sounded to indicate

the open door. We walked back down the colorless hallway and stood at the second door. We called out to the guard who was supposed to be there, but all we heard were the echoes of our own voices. We looked through the bars of the door and saw no one. Victoria was perfectly relaxed and explained that the prison was understaffed. The guards were making rounds, and every post was not always covered. We would have to wait until he came back.

I had not been nervous — but that was when I thought I could leave any time I wanted to. Suddenly, knowing I could not get past that door on my own, my view limited to the frame of metal bars, my departure dependent on the mercy of someone's return, eternal minutes passing, my anxiety increased. I kept reminding myself that the guard would return, that he would let us out. But there was something about realizing I had lost an element of control in this situation that was enormously unnerving.

In time — in what seemed like a very long time — the guard appeared, and we proceeded to make our way out of the prison.

Enclosed between two locked metal doors, I had been powerless. I had language; I had my own clothes; I had the confidence that justice would be served. And I could not imagine the physical absence of everything that made me feel human.

It is easy to feel pity for the one trapped behind visible and imposing bars. We feel sympathy; we call in psychologists; we diagnose reasonable, responsive behavior with terms like *post-traumatic stress*. We witness almost animalistic behavior at times as a human being resorts to employing basic instincts for pure survival. The scale has changed. They aren't even seeking happiness or gain or contentment; they just need to *survive*. Backed into the corners of cages, they are ready to brawl, ready to destroy anyone or anything that threatens their security.

For those who exist in an internal and relentless prison, we find it easier to come up with answers far more black-and-white. We can sentence another to a life we have not lived or experienced. Even when this must be so, it should be done with compassion and careful thought and an awareness that there are times when all that lies out there are two evils and the suffocating task of determining the lesser. This, I have found, is one of the hardest parts of learning about life. I assumed there would always be one right answer and one clearly wrong answer, and my task was just to recognize this fact and choose the right one. Life does not let us get away with something so formulaic, so elementary. It asks us to be more than that, to recognize something beyond our simplistic answers, but it does not rest just there. For in giving us the dilemma and the options, it affords us power. And in our chosen resolutions, we can preserve life, or we can crush the spirit of another trying to live it.

———

In the novel *The Agony and the Ecstasy*, full of quoteworthy literary gems, author Irving Stone describes a young Italian artist at age thirteen as he began his first apprenticeship. On one particular morning, Michelangelo did not go into the art studio as expected and instead walked to the beloved home of a stonecutter, Topolino, who was already engrossed in his task. As Michelangelo walked up to him, the teacher began to quietly narrate the work of his hands. He began with a caution, telling the young boy that the secret to stonecutting was to approach his stone "with friendliness, to seek its natural forms, its mountains and valleys, even though it might seem solid; never to grow angry or unsympathetic toward the material."

Topolino continued: "Stone works with you. It reveals itself.

But you must strike it right. Stone does not resent the chisel. It is not being violated. Its nature is to change. Each stone has its own character. It must be understood. Handle it carefully, or it will shatter. Never let stone destroy itself.... The power and the durability lay in the stone, not in the arms or tools."[6]

The stone was master, and not the mason, cautioned the wise instructor. And if ever a mason came to think he was master, the stone would oppose and resist him. One thing could be guaranteed: should a mason beat his stone in the way an ignorant contadino might beat his beasts, the rich, warm, glowing, breathing material would become dull and colorless. Even ugly. It would, in fact, die under his hand.

If treated with kicks and curses, with disdain and recklessness, this lifeless material will create an impenetrable veil around its soft inner core. It can be "smashed by violence but never forced to fulfill," Topolino declared with grave insight. In contrast, it yields to sympathy and grows more luminous and sparkling, its composition graced by fluid forms and symmetry.[7]

Violence comes in obvious forms — in yellow and purple bruises and shattered bones. We may recognize it in the harshness of words or the impact of a clenched fist. Yet it is beastly and equally harmful — I would argue perhaps even more harmful — in its less dramatically obvious forms: in cruelty and in crushing the confidence and self-respect rightfully carried by another.

And then, what of carelessness, where the essence and spirit of a human being are compromised and manipulated for our purposes? Is that not also a violation of another? Is this not its own form of violence? This is truly sobering, for it is harder to recognize, in ourselves as instigators, in an act we can inflict on another even in the absence of evil motives.

It is what we can do to another in romantic love when we try to make them into something they are not, when we love them for our own sake and not their sake. It is a violation of another, and of love itself. It is also what we can do in the name of ministry when we try to shape someone into God's calling on *our* lives, into what *we* think she should be and because of what *we* have done for her. We sing "To God Be the Glory," but threaded within our words and the way we continually tell her story is "to ourselves be the glory; great things we have done; and many are the people we have rescued."

When a girl is able to leave prostitution, she likely had someone to support and help her, and she will be the first to say she couldn't have done it alone. But any ministry must be careful not to inadvertently place an obligation on her. "We did help her, after all," the ministry may reason. Rather than releasing her to discover her own purpose, we can sometimes be quick to define it for her — with good intentions, of course. And more often than not, we will be tempted to guide her toward our own purpose for her. "She owes it to us and to other women like herself," we might think.

Yet her calling might be entirely different from ours. It makes sense to us, and we are often so committed to our own passions that we neglect to allow another the freedom and space to discover her own. Unintentionally, we can repeat a pattern of exploitation in the life of one who will easily fall into this familiar dynamic and claim the place that is hers in this new relationship — the lesser, smaller place of one who is indebted and constantly called to look back on when she was lifeless — instead of recognizing who she has become. But this time, we use the name of God to give weight to what may well be *our* will for her life.

We are given the privilege and the opportunity to participate in her life. And implicit in the opportunity lies significant responsibility. For if we beat the stone with our own reflection, even into the worthy callings that God gave to *us*, what once carried potential to be warm and glowing will instead become dull and colorless. *You can bruise and even kill it, but you cannot force it to fulfill.*

Now to her who seeks its natural forms, its mountains and valleys; who recognizes its beauty, its depth and its breadth, and calls it to live into what it already possesses, she will witness the grand fulfillment of what lay therein, the divine essence and calling of a wonder and creation that reflects something miraculous — a reflection of God himself.

chapter 8

perceptions

Wreaths of green illuminated by white twinkle lights were perched atop every doorway. When it nears the end, winter speaks to me of brown slush and cumbersome coats. But at its onset, brisk air is a catalyst for rosy cheeks, for nights warmed by hot cocoa topped with plump marshmallows, and the sense of something magical.

"There is a decorated Christmas tree in the event room," the man standing in the doorway to my office stated.

"That is ... a problem?" I asked.

"It's a Hanukkah party."

"Ah." I nodded my head in agreement. That was a problem.

My heels clicked along the marble floor as I walked the long corridor to reach the winding staircase. I passed large portraits of the president and the vice president of the United States and ornate doors into offices that were shared by two, three, or four people.

It was fall 2002, one year after the fateful day of September 11 when two hijacked planes crashed into the Twin Towers in New York City. A third crashed into the Pentagon, and a fourth crashed into an open field in Pennsylvania. More than 2,700 people were killed, and the heart of America was the target — its people, halls of government, and symbols of financial stability intrinsic to a world superpower. To protect against another terrorist attack, all the offices along the street side of the historic Old Executive Office building on Pennsylvania Avenue had been vacated. Interns, directors, and appointees piled into shared offices.

Several offices had fireplaces that were original to the building, and though it had been years since embers last glowed in their caves, they warmed up any room. Inside each office was a mini world that spilled into the hallways and the global sphere itself. The sounds of voices and high heels reverberated off the high ceilings, the sounds of an ever-present energy.

The beauty of the building never escaped me as I entered its lobby and scanned my badge, waited for the click of the turnstile, dropped my messenger bag on the belt, and walked through the metal detector. I waved to the familiar security guard, who was about six foot five and stood in stern observation, unless he knew you. Then he broke into a friendly grin as you passed by — after the green light flashed, of course.

At twenty-four years old, I was one of the oldest interns at the White House in Washington, D.C. I loved being in the center of information and current events. I thrived in the way it challenged me, in the fast pace and feeling of accomplishment when I was given a task that no one explained how to do but had every expectation I should and would figure out how to complete. There was no room for error; everything mattered, lending intensity to even the most mundane tasks. Thus a twelve-hour day passed by in what seemed to be minutes.

I was on a three-month term in the Office of Public Liaison, the point of contact for all citizen or constituency groups. It never ceased to amuse me when I answered the phone and heard a common request: "Hi, I live in [insert state] and would like to speak to the president."

He's a little busy right now with running the country and all. He'll get back to you shortly. That is how I responded in my head anyway.

One of my responsibilities was to help organize briefings on various issues, such as homeland security, Medicare, education, and international women's issues. I enjoyed them all and learned some of the intricacies of wildly debated current initiatives. I learned that whether a bill was passed or not, the phones rang off the hook the next day from an angry 50 percent.

It was the special interest group of international women's and children's issues that redefined my personal goals and ambitions. I remember standing along the back wall of the meeting room one day and seeing twenty-five women from Afghanistan in the blue theater seats of the front row. They were there by invitation of the administration and would be completing a computer course and technical training before returning to their country with new skills for employment. Everyone spoke in hushed tones. I surveyed the room from the back wall, clutching my notepad firmly and fidgeting with the silver chain of the ID card around my neck.

The president walked onto the stage and gave a word of greeting. In typical form, he opted to move from behind the podium and engage with his audience. When he stepped down, no one was prepared for what happened.

He intended to shake the hands of his guests, women who had endured much in their war-torn country, and not just from the blasts of bombs. But it was not a hand they offered in return. They dropped to their knees and literally bowed in an emotional display of gratitude as tears ran down their faces. They kissed their fingertips and reached out to touch his shoes.

The president was surprised, and while obviously stirred, he was also visibly uncomfortable and immediately tried to encourage them to stand up. It was a respect he believed they were long overdue.

The story did not make the evening news, since no media were allowed to record the event. But I was deeply affected by the picture of women being handed the respect and opportunity that were painfully unfamiliar.

When my internship concluded, I knew I wanted to focus on this global field. As a woman, I felt a responsibility to be a voice for fellow women whose voices were being silenced. As a human being, I felt drawn to the opportunity to reach out to those who were most vulnerable, a fragment of global society where women and children were often victimized — both because of what had been done to them and because of what people saw when they looked *at* them instead of *in* them. I wanted to look inside, to really see them. I wanted to speak louder than the voices that had told them they were anything less than invaluable.

I began to research global needs and evaluate the methods and operational integrity of organizations that were seeking to meet that need. I envisioned blazing my own trail, an independent path outside of the family ministry. I considered a position I had been offered with the Justice Department. It looked like it would have been perfect, but something didn't fit. As it turned out, vision and passion aligned — and the best place to pursue my dream was right in front of me. I declined the offer that carried prestige and recognition and returned to Atlanta to accept an unparalleled opportunity at Wellspring International.

———

It took over two hours to navigate the Pakistani airport upon arrival. With my head covered and suitcase in tow, I finally walked through the exit at two in the morning. I had arrived from Dubai on the same plane as the national cricket team that was arriving home after making their country proud. I walked outside to a mass of people, flashbulbs, and paparazzi. I already wondered how I would recognize the Canadian couple I had never met, and the party at the airport didn't make it any easier, but thankfully they found me.

As we arrived at their flat, they spoke Urdu in quiet tones with trusted local friends, holding a hand up to guess my height and pinching their hands around my waist. I was going to need a salwar kameez, the traditional dress for women, so as to not draw any negative attention. Salwar are loosely fitting, pajama-like trousers, and the kameez is like a long shirt, or tunic. In Pakistan, women wear a salwar kameez in every color — striking jewel tones of blues and reds. A matching dupatta, or long shawl, is worn as a scarf in more relaxed regions and as a head covering in conservative areas. For the first few days, I would wear the scarf around my neck before driving to the Northwest Frontier, where the dupatta would hide everything except my eyes. A few hours before the sun came up, I said good night and settled into my room. After a quick shower, I reached into my suitcase and found a pair of drawstring pants and a shirt that didn't match. I crawled between the clean sheets to take an oft-disrupted nap, waking up each time the power cut off and stilled the fan as the heat settled on me like a wet blanket.

My hostess, Jane, softly knocked on my door a few hours later to awaken me for breakfast. Over scrambled eggs and toast, she and her husband told me about the day trip they set up to go to the Indian border to see the changing of the guard. It was a fantastic experience, they said, and they were right.

It was an hour-long drive, with five adults and four children piled into a compact SUV. The man in the driver's seat was Jacob. I had just met him and his wife, Farah, along with their three young boys, ages ten, nine, and eight. He could communicate in English, and his sons did quite well in the language too. Their cousin came along too, and the boys had claimed the rear seat and found a way to roughhouse despite the cramped wrestling ring. The air-conditioning in the car struggled to keep up with the 125-degree temperature, but the heat was so intense that it was nauseating. We tried rolling down the windows, but waves of dust kicking up from the tires blew into our eyes.

One of the boys started to call out in Urdu to Farah, and she scrambled around to find something. I wasn't sure what she was looking for — until a few seconds later when she didn't find it. The little guy launched the contents of his stomach onto the floor of the car, while the rest of us turned in the direction of the closest window. I scrunched my eyes closed and tried to breathe through my mouth.

I turned around to look at him sympathetically, and he wiped his mouth with the back of his hand, blinked his eyes a few times, and looked up at me with a dimpled grin.

We arrived at the border where a single measured foot distinguished one person as a Pakistani and another as an Indian. Farah motioned to me to pull the dupatta over my head.

We walked toward the stadium, and I was amused to see the little guy who had been sick running around in childlike freedom, completely undeterred by vomit stains on both pant legs.

Once through the security checkpoint (men on one side and

women on the other), we sat on bleachers. Behind me were rows and rows of women, a striking picture of color, with shades of orange, pink, and green blending together against the backdrop of the bright blue sky. Across from me sat hundreds of men in their traditional shades of white or brown.

Soon an armed soldier stood above us on a decorated bridge. He presented a striking picture as he stood with perfect posture in a pristine, black military uniform with gold buttons and accents of red. His hat was a black cap fitted to his head at the base. There was a wide band of red fabric around the circumference, and a black tail of fabric hung down his back. Out of the top of the hat sprung tall black bristles that fanned out dramatically over his head. He raised an arm and began to chant loudly, "ZINDABAD! PAKISTAN!" The crowd roared in response, joining the chant with fervor: "LONG LIVE! PAKISTAN!"

I looked at the gates to my left, knowing that the other side was filled with people on bleachers, lifting their voices to chant with equal fervor for India. It was quite a remarkable sight, and the zealous political passion stirred a sense of acute awareness. After much procession, a contingent of guards marched before us in a perfectly synchronized drill of steps, turns, and switching of guns from one shoulder to the other. Then, one lone guard began a slow, dramatic march forward. The gates slowly opened, and he soon stood chest to chest with a guard wearing the brown uniform and gold medals for India. After an extended stare, they backed off from each other as choreographed; each took several individual turns and marching steps, again met chest to chest, and with a final spin marched back to their respective sides while their citizens roared.

Though they are as close as a border line, the typical build of a Pakistani man was so different from the slender build of a typical Indian man. When I stepped down from the bleachers, I was face-to-face with a gold button on a black uniform. I think it was near his belly button. I lifted my head to look up, up, up until my neck was stretched all the way back against my shoulders. His crisp black eyes stared down at me. His chiseled bone structure was set in a firm expression; his broad shoulders made me feel either safe or intimidated. He was quite the imposing figure and stood at about six foot seven. One of the boys ran from behind me and sidled up next to him, slipping his little hand into the giant-sized one. The guard looked down at him and closed his hand around the smaller one as they walked toward the exit. They had never met before.

I climbed back into the middle seat of the car. The little guy who had been sick was now sitting on the console between the two front seats, but facing into the backseat. He was so cute, and we sat face-to-face the whole trip home, his dimpled grin staring at me as his chin rested in his hands. The unrelenting odor of his soiled jeans in such close proximity made for a memorable ride home.

In the apartment below Steve and Jane lived a gentleman named Aasim and his family. He was in his thirties and worked full-time to help manage the house for Steve and Jane. He did the grocery shopping, cleaned the kitchen, and took care of the grounds, while his little son and daughter played, running along behind him. He was reserved, and even though we could communicate only a little, I could tell he was extremely intelligent. He spoke some English and was quite mysterious, but he had a good sense of humor. I was sitting at the kitchen table with my open notebook to review Urdu words I had scribbled down as I heard them. Trying to read my poor penmanship, I pronounced one of the words out loud to myself. I heard a laugh escape him and looked up to see him shake his head, with a twinkle in his eye and an amused grin on his face. Clearly I had not nailed the pronunciation.

I was leaving to go to the North-West Frontier Province at 11:00 p.m. the following day. Jacob, Farah, and their oldest son would travel with me all night to take me to the area just outside Swat Valley and the Taliban stronghold, where thousands of people live in displacement camps. But on the day of departure there was a problem. The air-conditioning in the car stopped working. "We cannot afford to fix it," Jacob said soberly. "No problem," I assured him. "I can do without." Adamantly, he shook his head no. The heat was far too intense — so intense I had probably never felt anything like it — and it would be a five-hour drive. It was not healthy, he said.

I set out to find an ATM machine and $200. Several blocks and four machines later, my hopes finally came to fruition as I found one that worked, and I exhaled loudly when I heard that glorious humming sound as it dispensed my cash, keeping my departure time on schedule.

As daylight gave way to darkness, I finished dinner and went to my room to pack into my backpack a change of clothes and the passport I hoped I would not be asked to reveal. I showered and put on borrowed clothes that were a perfect fit. I draped the soft, pink dupatta loosely over my head and threw the tail of fabric over the back of my left shoulder. I slipped a pair of gold sandals on my feet, slung the backpack over my shoulder, and was ready to go. Officially speaking.

I had not expected to feel nervous, but as the clock hands inched closer to 11:00 p.m., I felt butterflies stirring in my stomach. Jane handed me two canteens filled with cold water, and I added them to the bottles I had thrown into my bag. "You keep drinking water," she cautioned.

Aasim walked out of the kitchen with what could have been interpreted as a concerned expression and handed me an egg sandwich he had just made and carefully wrapped. It was for the car trip, he said. Jane took my face in her hands and kissed my cheek. As we pulled away, I looked back to see them standing in the street, their silhouettes waving good-bye through the darkness.

I settled into a corner of the backseat, took a sip of water from the canteen, and tried to calm my stirring nerves. I was a little disappointed in myself, as I didn't normally feel apprehensive or worry about safety. It's not that I am foolish. I always took precautions, but then I usually moved forward without hesitation. I really wanted to be here and even neglected to mention my destination to my father because I didn't want to create any concern that might hinder the trip. Part of my responsibility for Wellspring is to find areas of legitimate need and identify projects to help meet those needs. I had read books and articles on the current situation and possessed a deeply rooted desire to witness the need of epic proportion and hopefully identify a way for Wellspring to provide a helpful response.

It is difficult to quantify and rank various states of emergencies that simultaneously occur around the world. But the escalating numbers in this situation set it apart from various other conflicts. Over two million people had been displaced in the course of two months due to fighting between the Taliban and the Pakistani military forces. They had gathered in IDP (Internally Displaced Persons) camps in Mardan, about thirty miles from Swat Valley and the Taliban stronghold. The road that led into the valley cut through the center of the city and allowed access with relative ease. As opposed to refugees, these are people who stay within the boundaries of their own country. They have citizenship, but no home. Their homes — houses they owned on land they cultivated — stood in a path of fatal destruction as the fighting continued. They fled with the clothes on their backs, some leaving behind missing family members, or the sight of their houses ablaze or demolished by gunfire and grenades. Now they were living in canvas tents that had been donated by an aid organization, or they had claimed the corner of a schoolroom, among hundreds of thousands of other people like them.

Blend in, everyone had urged. Foreigners were advised not to be here. My dark hair and dark eyes could blend in well enough, but I was worried that my unfamiliarity showed in the way I carried my veil. It was uncomfortable. I couldn't see properly, and I was aware of limitations in breathing. Rather than a full breath drawn in and exhaled with instinctive ease, the air itself was limited.

There was also my inability to speak the language. In this single way, being a woman served me well, for my silent observation would go unnoticed, even preferred. As we traveled, Jacob set out to teach me important answers to give should I be asked certain questions. The syllables were unfamiliar to me, and although I tried to mimic their sounds, I was failing miserably. "No," he shook his head with a bit of frustration. "You must get the accent right!" My belief that I could "blend in" began to wane. Our confidence lay in 50 percent of my DNA, my South Asian genes and appearance, given to me by the father who had no idea where I actually was.

Around 2:00 a.m., Jacob pulled over to the side of the road. I sat up alertly and inquired what he was doing. He said he needed to take a nap because he was falling asleep at the wheel. I really wanted him to try to stay awake. I really wanted him to keep driving. And I really really wanted him to stay in the car. As a guest, and as a woman, I felt limited in my protest. I was aware that both of those things also took away the freedom to exit the vehicle alone once he left.

He propped open the hood to cool the engine and walked several paces over to a grassy area to lie down. Much to my chagrin, I was frightened. What if someone came to the car while he was gone? I tried to remember the sentences he had taught me. By now I had forgotten both the accent and the words.

Unfortunately, I have read too many news articles for my own good. Stories of kidnappings now played cruelly with my mind, and I began to envision all kinds of scenarios, with only darkness and silence to aggravate my worries. I have often called my sister "Wilson," after the volleyball in *Castaway* that kept Tom Hanks sane and comforted on his deserted island far from home. On any continent, whether it is home or on the other side of the world, in any circumstance — from having hurt feelings because a salesclerk snapped at me to being on the side of the road at 2:00 a.m. in a high-conflict area — she is my voice of calm. I held my BlackBerry in my hand to key into her calm and watched the green numbers on the digital clock change every minute for an hour and half. Jacob returned, and we were on our way.

Finally, my heavy eyelids stuttered to a close — for a few quiet minutes — until I was awakened sharply as my head slammed against the window. Our backup driver had been fighting against his own drooping eyelids, and they had won. The car slammed into the median and scraped along its side, but he quickly regained control. Farah's son whimpered and I rubbed the dull ache in my left temple, but we continued driving, and I was soon distracted by the sunrise against a backdrop of rocky mountainous terrain.

We were nearing the heart of the war zone and the Taliban regime.

"What happens if they find Americans?" I asked.

"They are usually kidnapped and held hostage," Jacob answered plainly. I thought it was better if I didn't ask too many more questions.

As we pulled off the quiet roads into signs of life and activity, Farah began carefully adjusting the covering for my head and face. "It must not come loose," she stated emphatically. I forgot my earlier decision regarding questions and asked what would happen if it did. "You will have acid thrown on your face," came Jacob's reply. I freed a hand to pull it tighter. The *niqab* was a single piece of fabric that lay over my head. I let it fall to cover my forehead and the sides were tucked behind my ears. Farah taught me to reach my right hand across my body to take hold of the left side of the veil. I brought it over my left ear, under my eye, across the bridge of my nose, and across the other side of my face. It was secured behind my right ear, and the right side of the veil hung down over the top. All that was exposed were the colors of my eyes and my sandaled feet.

I exited the car when told to do so and started to follow, but my limited peripheral vision made it surprisingly difficult.

"It's OK, sister. Follow me this way," said the small voice I recognized. At ten years old, Joshua was this little man with a short, stocky build. He appointed himself to be my guardian, and I was sincerely grateful. He was my eyes, and he seemed to sensitively see into the thoughts that my mind was so thoroughly covering.

I heard the story of a man who had been kidnapped by the Taliban the previous year. I learned in detail that he was hung from a ceiling and tortured. I heard of his miraculous escape and his return home to his wife and one-year-old child — the little girl who sat on my lap, with honey-colored ringlets across her forehead and round hazel eyes looking up at me, seemingly unconcerned that I did not look familiar.

I stepped into Internally Displaced Persons (IDP) camps and dynamics I had not encountered in other camps elsewhere. The political tensions were high, and the response from the international community had been lacking. The reasons were not simple, but the need was significant. In moments, dozens of women and a plethora of voices surrounded me. They were all speaking at once, each in a language I could not understand. I looked down at Joshua, who leaned in to listen and translate what each one said.

Are you here to help us?
We don't have any vegetables.
We have lost our homes.
Where are you from?
Are you an American?
Can you get us some vegetables?

Everyone had lost something. A husband, a mother, a child, their home, their sense of security, their self-sufficiency. In the presence of women alone, I had let the headscarf fall to my shoulders, exposing my damp hairline and flushed cheeks. As we turned to leave, I started to draw it back onto my head but paused when my eyes caught a flash of red. I looked to see her standing in her strawberry red salwar kameez against the white-wash of the schoolroom in a positively striking picture. She was about twelve years old, and she smiled shyly as she waved her hand to say hello. I walked over, and her green eyes lit up. Her name was Rubelina. I asked her where her family was, and with a sad expression, she just shook her head. But she pointed to a mini version of herself and said, "Sister." Hearing her name, her mini-me ran over and cuddled up beside her. I really, really wanted to get them vegetables — and so much more.

At another camp I walked down dusty rows of burlap tents, where the presence of 25,000 people called forth a near silence. I walked past the suspicious eyes of an elderly man who was crouching on the ground outside his tent, an aluminum plate sitting empty beside him.

"We have no vegetables," another man said to me in English.

At one time, they had a single doctor from the UK. But women can only be seen by a female doctor. Women are limited in their education in this region, so female doctors are scarce, and pregnant women were not receiving medical attention. The male doctor could, however, treat the men and the children. But the previous week, he stepped out of his tent one day and was not wearing a salwar kameez. A vigilant protestor shot him point-blank in the head. Now they had no doctor.

The Western world was doing nothing, a man living in the camp said with fervor. I motioned to the white humanitarian aid banners nearby, the only signs I could see. But he shook his head no. They were local branches, he said. They had nothing to do with the Western world. I could not protest — but not because I had no information to the contrary.

It was true that the few aid organizations there were in danger of leaving. Given the hotspot of tensions reverberating around the world, it had become increasingly difficult to raise financial support for aid to this region because donors had grown afraid they were somehow funding terrorist activity rather than, say, rice. Aid organizations fought to reduce the stigma, but they could not raise enough money to allow them to stay.

I asked what they needed most, though so many needs were obvious. Their houses. Their mothers. Their independence. Their sense of security. Their land. Clean water. Medical treatment. Privacy. Sanitation. Enough food. Peace.

"Could you try to get us some vegetables?" they asked.

Here I spent some time with a government worker, who was both helpful and gracious. He explained their situation and the food provisions from the United Nations' World Food Programme, but there just wasn't enough to go around, given the sheer number of people they were trying to help. He jotted his phone number on a card and handed it to me. I asked him about vegetables. "This is a luxury we cannot afford right now," he told me.

When it was time to leave, Jacob turned the engine, but it sputtered and then lapsed into silence. After several attempts, he stepped out, motioning with his hand that Farah and I needed to stay inside. The windows were rolled up. The thermometer read 125 degrees, and we were confined in a vacuum of heat. I could feel sweat pouring down my spine. I tried to shift the veil, but I wanted so badly to lift it over my head and take in a big gulp of air. Farah sat very still but seemed unconcerned. I could not speak Urdu, and she could not speak English, but she had watched me all day with the concern of a mother, reassuring my thinly veiled confusion with a nod of her head. The corners of her eyes turned up again in a smile, and I concluded that she had the patience of Job.

I lost all sense of time, but eventually, and thankfully while we were still conscious, Jacob opened his door and let in a welcomed wave of air, albeit thick and humid. He slid in front of the steering wheel and turned the key again. The engine sputtered and choked and released into a full start.

It had been a long day of confusion from every angle — how to dress, how to behave, how to ask questions, how to find any conceivable solution to problems ranging from vegetables to international relations. After midnight, we piled in for the last time to make the long drive back south. We were making our way along the ominous road, the territory of the Taliban just on the other side. Jacob slowed down and pulled to the side of the road. He propped open the hood and walked away in the darkness to what I imagined was a grassy mat. The car was silent except for the sounds of deep breathing.

I quietly rummaged through my bag to entertain myself. A roll of toilet paper, a small bottle of Purell hand sanitizer — nothing that would entertain me for long. Then I found a roll of breath mints and a bottle of warm water. I settled back into the seat and guzzled the water in one gulp and snacked on peppermints. Two hours later, we were on our way.

Another hour down the road, Jacob pulled off into a rest stop. He had a headache, he said. He was going to need to stop for a while. I produced a bottle of Advil and a hope-filled smile.

At 6:30 a.m., we pulled up to the house, where Aasim stood outside, watching and waiting. For me. As I stepped out of the car, he nodded his head with satisfaction and reached for my backpack. I said good-bye to Jacob and Farah. My guardian angel, Joshua, was sleeping, and I brushed my hand across his forehead and whispered thanks — in his language this time.

I had been awake for the better part of forty-eight hours, but I went straight for a shower, letting the hot water run down my face (soaring temperatures kept the pipes nice and toasty, even if I turned the knob to the "cold" setting). Then I crumpled into bed.

A knock on the door stirred me awake a few hours later. It was almost noon. "You should have something to eat," Rachel said softly. Rachel also worked in the home, managing the laundry and cooking.

"Do you think you could teach me how to make chapatis?" I asked hesitantly.

She broke into a smile and nodded her head. We stood in the kitchen, the hottest part of the house because of the heat from frying pans and the oven.

Shaping the dough into a ball, she rolled it against her left palm, using her right hand to carefully mold it. Occasionally she would reach for a pinch of flour, never breaking the steady rhythm of shaping the dough, slowly transforming it into a flat pancake against her hand. Then she tossed it back and forth quickly between each palm, faster than the eye could follow. It was like she was counting in her head, for she stopped at the perfect time. It formed a proportional circle, with paper-thin thickness and perfectly intact. A single toss more and it would have crumbled in her hands, as it did in mine. She smiled and handed me a new ball of dough. "Again," she encouraged.

I loved feeling the chapati dough between my hands. I loved being able to shape something, and I loved the fact that she was undaunted when I needed to start over — how instead of demoting me to watch, she handed me a new ball of dough and seemed confident that I would do better. *Again and again.*

When she tossed each chapati into the frying pan, some were pathetic-looking circles and some inched closer to something right — and she made use of them all. And somewhere in there, I couldn't tell where, was a ball of dough I had ruined. She didn't throw it away. It had gone back into the bowl, and we shaped it into something new.

After my cooking lesson, I decided it would be wise to get off my feet, which had swelled quite unattractively in the last few days from the heat. I couldn't squeeze my size six feet into a single pair of sandals. I felt like one of Cinderella's stepsisters, their chubby feet stubbornly refusing to slide into a slipper and protruding over the edge before they snapped out like a rubber band. I settled on the sofa with a book in hand, grateful for all the day's experiences that I needed to process. Just as I began to open the book, I heard Rachel coming out of the kitchen, carrying a red plastic basin filled with water.

She crouched on the ground, placing the basin at my feet. I had not said anything about my feet, but she pointed at them as I tried to tuck them under the sofa. "It is not good," she said. "You need the salt water." In my embarrassment, I protested. "You are too good to be taking care of my ugly feet," I told her. But she only nodded and lifted each foot carefully off the floor and lowered it into the warm, soothing water. My feet were dusty, swollen, and quite unattractive.

She scooped up water with her hand and poured it over my toes, making sure my enlarged ankles were doused. She massaged them with her hands, encouraging blood flow. "You must sit here for a while," she said, gently patting my knee the way a mother does endearingly to her child. She stood up, adjusted the silk threads of her salwar, and went back to her work in the kitchen.

I came to offer something, to fix something. Instead, a woman I had just met accepted me into her country and her life, kneeled down, and washed my feet.

The next morning, I dressed in a long peasant skirt that loosely brushed the floor, a long-sleeved T-shirt, and an ivory pashmina draped loosely over my head, and I went to board a plane. Hours later, I stepped off into the Dubai airport for a long layover. I walked into the bathroom to transform myself with a pair of jeans and ballet flats I had grabbed from my bag. I slipped into their comfort and stepped back outside. I boarded my next flight to London, and as it lowered onto the runway, I pulled up the shade to look out the window. The plane slowly taxied to the Jetway and came to a halt. Everyone immediately stood up to stretch arms and legs that had been uncomfortably twisted into faded seats. Slowly, passengers disembarked, and eventually I stepped off the plane, feeling the rush of cool air against my face. I let the pashmina fall to my shoulders and evolve to a scarf and quickened my step through the bridge that would put me on solid ground.

After clearing immigration and customs, I stepped through the double doors into the energy of Heathrow Airport. A man brushed quickly past me in a hurry to get somewhere. As he did so, he looked back over his shoulder to offer a quick apology. I was taken aback, and I stopped in my tracks to absorb the feeling. I ran a free hand through the hair that fell loosely to my shoulders. I breathed it in — the opportunity to feel fully present in the space around me. I was exposed. I was seen. Not the kind of being seen that is tinged with embarrassment. The kind that is characterized by freedom.

I wanted to recognize freedom, to honor it, to realize what it offered instead of blazing through unaware and on a mission to retrieve, always, something else. I could not give it to Rubelina or the families confined to an IDP camp. I could honor them by not taking it for granted, but I couldn't present it to them. Not alone, and not in a day.

Of course, they didn't even ask me to do that. They just asked for vegetables. I would start there, but not settle for it. I'm confident that twenty-five women from Afghanistan didn't know they would stand in the White House one day, or that they would obtain computer efficiency certificates in the United States either.

Respect and freedom were always worth fighting for. I've seen American aid workers respond to the absence of it elsewhere with contempt for the freedom that is present in our home country. But guilt or resentment for the voice I did have certainly wouldn't help anyone.

I could, however, use this voice to try to make a difference. *Again and again.*

chapter 9

enduring

"Sorrow ... turns out to be not a state but a process," penned C. S. Lewis in his book *A Grief Observed*.[8] He wrote the account of his process after the death of his beloved wife in an honest portrayal of raw heartache, anger, and disillusionment — and ultimately of resolve. A wound that eventually seals into a scar is the physical equivalent of the internal process called grief. Or what we can know as grief. It is a significant part of the human experience — one we painfully seek to eliminate, bypass, cover over, ignore, and turn off with enough faith or by using the discipline of mind over matter.

We resist its outworking in our own lives, and often it is even more painful to look on it in the face of another. We want to intervene, to spare them from that undetermined place of unspecified ending.

The first time I had met Anna, I was staying in her house while visiting a potential project for work. I felt like I knew her as soon as she embraced me, which was as soon as she saw me. A missionary in a foreign land, she had been far away from home for years. She was in her early sixties, petite in form and genuinely sweet. She told me she had a bit of a wild streak when she was young, and after graduating from college, she joined the Peace

Corps and left her home in Scotland to live in South America for two years. Given the gentle voice and gracious manner I had just encountered, I smiled to learn she had always been full of surprises.

On her Peace Corps assignment, Anna taught at a girls' school. She had never been in South America and only spoke English, but she quickly learned how to speak Spanish and fry plantains. Another teacher repeatedly talked to her about God and invited her to church. Anna resisted her attempts for months, even with exasperation, but eventually, for a reason she was not sure of, she agreed to go to church. During that first day in church, she felt the presence of God in a way she believed she could not deny.

Anna returned home to attend a Bible college in preparation for returning to South America as a missionary. She planned to go alone, preferring the idea of her singular calling and independent ministry. But then she met the man who would become her husband and be part of a larger shared dream to return to South America together.

Life was hectic, with classes and studies and a new marriage, and as the pomp and circumstance of graduation neared, she was consumed by plans to return to the country she was inexplicably drawn to. Normally full of energy, she began to feel fatigued. The next day it was the same, with the addition of nausea. Anna soon learned she was pregnant, and she tried to wrap her mind around this big change in her life. It meant a necessary postponement of the overseas plans in preparation for the arrival of the little one. She was apprehensive, as it was all so new and the idea was still settling inside of her. During her first check-up, the doctor said to her, "You must be so thrilled!" She thought for a moment and broke into a sincere smile. "I really am," she answered honestly.

Months later, Anna gave birth to a healthy baby boy, and she and her husband named him Jonathan. The nurse in the delivery room was originally from South America, which seemed to be much more than a coincidence. As the beaming new mother looked at her tiny son, she proudly informed the nurse, "This baby is going to South America." She adored him and had never felt anything like the joy he brought into her life. She knew the sound of every cry, whether it meant he was hungry or tired or just wanted to be held in her arms. She sat in a rocking chair each night and held him close, singing the words to soft lullabies that soothed him to sleep. Plans continued for their departure, and Anna felt as if she was right in the center of where she was supposed to be, a place where everything was coming to fruition.

One Wednesday evening, with their Bible study group due to arrive at their home any minute, Anna busied herself with food preparation, stacking sandwiches on plates and pouring orange juice into a pitcher. Her friends started to arrive, and they greeted each other warmly with hugs and chatter about the week. They formed their chairs in a circle and began the study. As the dialogue continued, her internal clock told her it was time to wake Jonathan to feed him. She looked up at the dial on the wall to confirm she was right and quietly stood up, placing her Bible and notebook on her chair. Quietly, she slipped out and carefully turned the handle to go into Jonathan's room.

———

The e-mail spoke of Hama, a nineteen-year-old girl with kidney failure. She needed to be on dialysis, but her family could not afford it any longer. What she really needed was a kidney transplant. "Can Wellspring help her?" this guardian angel asked.

Hama was one of five children supported by her young widowed mother, Emilia, who worked as a tea lady. Her husband had died, and now her second child was sick. The thought of losing someone else in her family — her precious daughter — was terrifying to her. Emilia had undergone all of the necessary testing to see if her kidney was a match, but it wasn't, and neither was anyone else's in the family.

In Malaysia, by law only close family members could donate a kidney, and this left few options and minimal hope. As a result, there had been only five transplants in the whole country during the previous year — with twenty thousand patients waiting for transplants. Hama's mother had spent all of her money on medical costs and could no longer afford it. Without a funding source, the hospital could no longer provide care, and they had sent Hama home.

She was readmitted to the hospital when we contacted the office there and made arrangements to pay the outstanding bills. We sent her a bouquet of gerbera daisies, my favorite flowers. The first time I saw a picture of her, she was lying in her hospital bed, surrounded by her family and the red gerbera daisies. She was smiling.

Determined to find both a short-term and long-term solution, we contacted an organization in Malaysia called the National Kidney Foundation, an organ transplant and dialysis center that provided treatment for members of low-income families who cannot afford to go to private hospitals. They had recently initiated a patient adoption program, which enabled us to adopt her and pay the foundation each month for her dialysis treatments. On February 14, Hama went to the Foundation to receive her first treatment.

Three times a week for four hours at a time, this brave girl sat in a chair while blood was pumped out of her body through a machine, which did what her kidneys could not do for her, and then was pumped back into her body to continue to sustain her.

During my visit to Malaysia, I ate several meals in the home of this gracious Hindu family. They brought out a huge spread and insisted that I eat first. Emilia was a very sweet lady, and although she didn't speak English like her children, I felt we easily spoke volumes.

All of Hama's siblings were at the family meals, along with members of her extended family. I tried to remember all the new names. Her grandfather sat in front of the television, the sound blaring as we yelled back and forth to be heard over the din of the program.

"Did your father let you go to dance clubs when you were a teenager?" a cousin asked me, glaring at her father. I quickly deduced that I was coming in at the end of a conversation.

"Um, no," I replied. This made one of them happy. She didn't ask any other questions about the household rules I had as I was growing up.

After a huge dinner, it was time for dessert — a Southeast Asian fruit called durian. It is widely known, not so much for its taste as its smell. While it is a popular favorite, hotels will post signs in their windows reading, "NO DURIAN." Even before the fruit is cut open, it emits such a strong odor that it fills any room or car and remains for days. It is larger than a grapefruit or a mango, round or oblong in shape. The greenish-brown fruit is covered with little spikes, which, in my opinion, serves as a warning. Thus far, I had been able to avoid it on my visits to Asia, but this time my hosts were anxious to watch me taste it.

They had all gathered around, expectant looks on their faces and twinkles in their eyes. I looked at my audience and tentatively bit into the fruit. Immediately my face contorted and my eyes filled with tears. I shook my head, as if that would help me forget the taste, and they burst out laughing. The little girls clapped their hands and giggled in amusement.

As I got ready to leave later that night, Hama's mother shyly beckoned me into the kitchen and pulled a small box from behind her back. When I opened it, I saw a lovely gold necklace with blue stones. I shook my head that I couldn't accept this, but she took my hands in hers and held them so tightly. She couldn't speak, but she nodded her head yes, asking me to please receive what she could give.

When I returned home, my goal for Wellspring was to find a way to arrange for a kidney transplant. The dialysis treatments were going well, but Hama could not survive indefinitely like that. It was only a Band-Aid, and she needed something more. I mentioned her story during a presentation in the United States at a small gathering that Wellspring was hosting for potential financial supporters, and after the meeting, a gentleman came up to introduce himself. He shook my hand and handed me his card. He was a dialysis specialist from New Zealand, and he wanted to help Hama.

I put him in touch with the National Kidney Foundation in Malaysia to familiarize him with her particular needs, and then he set out on a mission. He made contacts with international specialists and clinics, while we raised funds. He identified a doctor, and a match was found. Medication was arranged to be donated. Within weeks, Hama was scheduled for her surgery abroad.

In July, I traveled to Hama's home in Kuala Lumpur to finalize arrangements and make sure all of their questions were answered. I delivered two airline tickets that had been purchased for her and her mother to depart in four weeks. An apartment had been arranged, as she needed to stay there for up to eight weeks for treatment and monitoring before returning home. The night before I left, we went out to dinner to celebrate. I remember where we sat. I can still see the smile on Hama's face, which had never left in all of those months, and her mother taking her face in my hands and saying the words she had practiced in English: "Thank you, with my heart."

"Why do you do this?" she had softly asked earlier that day as her niece translated. "Why in the world would a Christian organization single out a Hindu girl in another country who needs a kidney transplant?"

Later that night, as we lay awake in our twin beds, a good friend and colleague who had joined me said it best: "There are people all over the world who are needy, and they don't need to be reminded that they are needy. They need to be reminded that they matter. And nobody said that better than Christ. All the Hamas of the world need to know that."

Three weeks later, I was unable to reach Hama's family, and I was getting concerned. Late that night, I received a message.

———

As soon as Anna stepped inside Jonathan's room, she felt something was wrong. Chills ran down her spine as she walked over to the crib. She tried to stir him, and her cries turned into wailing as she realized her son would not awaken. She held Jonathan's tiny body in her arms as sobs spilled forth from the depths of her soul. She carried him to the living room, and holding him to her heart, she looked desperately at her husband through her tears, pleading for him to fix what she knew could not be restored. Wordlessly, her husband gently took Jonathan from her arms. He looked at his son's face, a face that resembled his own. He kissed the top of his head, and then he slowly, slowly raised his arms to lift the baby up to the heavens. Tears streamed down his cheeks as he lifted his eyes upward in an act of submission to a fate that broke his heart.

Anna cried out in protest. *No, no, no!* She was not ready to give him back to God. God had given him to her only months ago. He was an extension of her heart, born from her very flesh. She was not ready to part with him, not ready to accept what had been tragically forced on her.

And how could she? She was his mother. She had carried him inside of her for nine months. She had felt the exhilaration of her child's arrival into the world. She had held him, fed him, protected him, dreamed for him, cherished him. She would have given her very life for him.

Life would never again look the same. She couldn't bear to visit his grave for some time, but in a sense, she visited it every day. There may have been a site where marble was engraved for everyone else to see, but his life and death were engraved on her heart. In that way, he stayed with her.

People tried to comfort her, but there is no comfort for such a loss. In an effort to console her, they said, "You're young. You'll have other children." Perhaps, but she needed to grieve the loss of *this* child.

———

I tightened my grip around the handle of my office phone, punishing the instrument for the news it transmitted. Ten days before she was scheduled to leave for surgery, Hama had collapsed. Her heart stopped beating for six minutes, and though it rallied to beat once again, the rest of her body could not match its resilience, and the monitor next to her bed registered no brain activity.

Within days, Hama was taken off the ventilator, and her heart immediately rested.

That was four years ago, and I still don't know how to make sense of this story. We were so close. Everything had fallen into place, and I find it difficult to understand why Hama's story ended the way it did.

As I sit here now, flipping my pen through my fingers as if it will inspire some type of epiphany and answer my lingering question, I realize I am looking at a red gerbera daisy sitting in a vase on the table. I picked this one up at a little flower shop on my way home a few days ago, and suddenly I'm reminded of the one in Hama's picture.

Some people don't understand why someone would pay for a bouquet of flowers. Soon their petals will close, and only the memory of what once was, remains. I know this, and yet I still buy flowers. Maybe it is because in their fullness they bring such beauty to my day, a loveliness that softens me every time I am in their presence or reach out to feel their delicate petals between my fingers. Even as the colors of ruby red or golden yellow fade, they have changed the way I remember the space around me.

———

I find it difficult to cry in front of people, and I'm not even sure why. Even when I want to cry, I can't. Behind closed doors or on the bathroom floor (what is it about bathroom floors that lend themselves to be the cave of our emotional meltdowns?), I dissolve into a fountain of expression. But as I listened to Anna's story, mutinous tears escaped my eyes, and I made no effort to wipe them away. I ached inside for this woman who had suffered one of the greatest kinds of loss in life. How was she still so graciously soft instead of hardened with bitterness?

Over the years, Anna brought three more children into the world, but her family did not go to South America as they planned. Her dream of South America had included Jonathan, and the idea of going without him brought with it enormous pain that was too much to bear. Twenty years passed before she returned to it and began to carefully unwrap it again. I want to believe that God understood this. Somehow, for me, it would seem to uphold the integrity of grief.

Anna had allowed space for healing, for a process that is complicated and needs the grace of time for authenticity. She allowed it to bring her to a place where deep sorrow and a kind of peace learn to live together in the same heart. And when she was ready, she began to dream again.

But it was not to go to South America — that remained in a special place in her heart with Jonathan. It evolved into something of a different shape, and after the children were grown, she and her husband moved to a country she had never visited before.

Peace discovered will never minimize what was lost, but experiencing peace does afford us the ability to finally disengage from the battle of resisting what has already happened and what we cannot change. It is that place of acceptance called healing.

We sat now in her home in Central America, glasses of cold Sprite sweating in front of us. The power went off, and it only took seconds to feel waves of heat radiate through the room. But we made no effort to move. We heard footsteps outside, and the flip of the switch to start the generator. Slowly the fans began to hum to life.

I sat across from Anna as a guest in her home. She had shared with me her grief. And isn't your deepest pain the greatest gift you can give to anyone — when you slowly release the fingers from what you hold so tightly and invite someone into your vulnerability? I remembered a line from a beloved book, *Shanta-ram*. In the context of romantic relationships, author Gregory David Roberts wrote that shared wounds, when pinned to the sky, become stars in the night that help us navigate a pathway home.[9] It can be said of friendship as well.

Anna smiled sadly. Life had brought remarkable pain, but she spoke of its richness too. "Every now and then, God brings somebody incredibly special across your path. That's one of life's gems. You must remember those things and hold on to them," she said peacefully.

I wondered if she knew that she was one of those gems to me.

———

The gospel of John tells the story of the death of Lazarus, the brother of Martha and of Mary — the one who would later, with tears of joy, pour perfume on Jesus' feet and wipe them with her hair in an act of worship. Jesus would defend her and honor her. But first came another encounter.

Lazarus became sick, and the sisters immediately sent word to Jesus. They believed in him and knew he could do miracles. They must have thought he would come right away, but he didn't. He waited. And during that time, Lazarus died.

When the sisters heard that Jesus was finally coming, Martha ran out to meet him, but Mary stayed inside. I wonder if she felt betrayed. She had believed in him; she had called on him. But he seemingly ignored her. He didn't show up in time for something that meant life to her.

The Bible tells us that Martha returned inside and told Mary that Jesus was calling for her. Instantly, she stood up and ran out to him. I picture this wounded little girl, her head resting on a table, sobbing because her heart is hurting. She feels abandoned by the one person she put her faith in. She feels hurt, perhaps even angry. She hears that he is near, but she doesn't go to him. After all, he had forgotten about her.

But then she hears that he called for her by name, and she quickly goes to him. Maybe she knew that the one she had felt betrayed by was the only one who could comfort her. Maybe when Jesus called for her, she knew it meant that he had not forgotten her.

And so Mary goes to Jesus and falls at his feet, weeping. One day, she would fall at his feet in humility, knowing he had saved her, but first, she would fall at his feet, pouring out a broken heart, thinking he had betrayed her. She had experienced enormous loss — a loss that she believes he could have prevented. Jesus takes one look at her as she weeps, and the Bible tells us he was deeply troubled. And what did he do? He cried, even though he knew that life was about to be resurrected and her pain relieved. But first, he wept right along with her.

How much, then, would Jesus grieve with one who must endure loss? Would he also say, "Where have you put him?" And would she show him, not the grave, but her heart? And he would come and sit by this tomb and weep. For twenty years — for ever.

signs of life

One day last year, as I was going for a run, I saw a letter typed on an 8½" by 11" sheet of stark white paper plastered to the trunk of a forsaken tree.

Notice of Intent to Remove Street Trees

June 23, 2009

The Public Landscape Division of the Community Maintenance Department will be removing the following Carob (*Ceratonia siliqua*) trees located in the street right-of-way adjacent to 1117 10th Street and 1321 Hill Street.

Both trees display symptoms of advanced internal decay in their trunks and scaffold limbs, and overall their structural stability is in very poor condition. Fruiting bodies of sulfur fungus (*Ganoderma applanatum*), which indicates extensive internal decay, have been detected at the base of their trunks. This fungus destroys the internal structure of the tree, reducing the strength of the wood and the overall structural stability of the tree. As the decay has progressed, the potential of limb and/or trunk failure has increased, and it has been determined that both trees have high potential for failure.

The removals will begin in approximately 14 days from the date of this notice.

The replacement trees for the two individual sites are:

1117 10th Street will be a 36-inch box camphor (*Cinnamomum camphora*)

1321 Hill Street will be a 36-inch box Crape myrtle (*Lagerstroemia indica "Muskogee"*)

The replacement trees will be planted within 20 working days after the removals are complete.

I stood on an empty street, my hands on my hips and my jaw hanging open in despair, scanning my surroundings as if searching for someone to help. I surveyed the tree. It looked to be in decent shape and as if it had served its purpose as well as could be expected. There were visibly green leaves; the trunk looked solid; it seemed to have signs of life. I was offended that it was to be replaced by a presumably lovelier Crape myrtle, obviously one that didn't have signs of internal decay — yet.

Later that day, I escorted my sister over to the tree and passionately defended its existence, lamenting that it was being judged and deemed to be a failure just because of a little internal decay — and therefore sentenced to complete removal altogether. "I mean, who *doesn't* have a little internal decay?" I argued.

My sister seemed amused, and I knew she knew me well enough to know where all this was going. I was upset for the tree. I was upset because *I* was the tree, and this notice could have been plastered to *my* forehead.

Four months earlier, I had observed a birthday I will not forget. But it was not marked with laughter and toasts. It was sad and commemorated with tears. It had nothing to do with the extra candle on my cake or the additional number of silver strands invading my thick head of black hair, but rather an awareness of the passing of time and the absence of things I thought would be. Defining events ripped open floodgates to the past and to painful memories I had worked hard to disconnect from, pretending that they weren't really mine and that I did not have to feel their impact.

One year before, I had celebrated a momentous birthday, the welcomed launch into a new decade and simultaneously a new city. Two weeks before I turned thirty, I took a significant step I was certain would redefine my life and moved across the country. Doing so meant leaving behind some of the key relationships and things that had defined me thus far — my hometown, my family, my friends, and my job. I loaded up a few Hefty garbage bags of clothes, my guilty-pleasure flat-screen television, and my most prized possession — an eighty-five-pound golden retriever named India. Together, we set out on a new adventure in a city that boasted of palm trees, year-round blue skies, no need for air-conditioning — the place where dreams come true.

To be fair, it *did* have palm trees.

My excitement was quickly challenged by the details everyone confronts in a new city. I didn't know how to get anywhere. I didn't have anywhere to go. I had exchanged acreage and a house I could afford for a three hundred square foot space that I couldn't afford. These are the things that don't really matter over time.

The distance of miles took its toll on friendships back home for reasons I recognized but did not completely understand. I couldn't find a place where I fit; who I was did not seem to be enough to fill the spaces around me. There is a difference between aloneness and loneliness. I did not fear being alone; but I felt painfully lonely. These are the details that hover in darkening shades of gray over time to make way for a storm. As the clock slowly ticked by, the skies above were not clearing, and in time, they poured forth a perfect storm.

It wasn't a single event or the fault of a single person. It was a series of events that all spelled loss, and with a final straw of disappointment, I imploded. Sometimes you think you have already hit bottom, only to find there are miles left to go; there's bottom, like a hundred feet of debris, and then somewhere after that you set up camp. I tried to breathe, and with childlike frailty I said prayers of pleading that this was now truly the bottom. I so vividly remember lying on the pleather sofa in my apartment, painfully aware of the deafening sound of a silence to life, one that I had not heard before. I had made the sofa my bed, my desk, my coffee shop, my conference room. I think I took bathroom breaks. In one particular moment, my eyes were closed, and I clearly heard someone whisper my name. I flashed open my eyes and scanned the room, pleading to see someone, but no one was there. I slowly closed my eyes and begged for sleep to visit me again.

My father came for an unexpected visit and tactfully asked when I had last showered. My eager-to-please golden retriever sighed heavily one night before she climbed up once again to share the crowded sofa space with me, imploring me with expressive eyes to consider making my way back to the mattress on the floor in the next room.

Weeks turned into months, and then, little by little, the storm abated. As it slowed to a drizzle, I would not say I was met with happiness. But I do believe I made peace with all that contributed to the raging thunder. Or is that why it slowed to a drizzle? I can't be sure. When I look back on that year, I left home believing I was looking for a fresh start, while in reality I had also been looking for a soft place to fall. But the distance of some falls is so far that it won't allow for any kind of buffer. Some heartache is so great that the only way out is by plunging into its chaos. And some loss is so significant that your heart will shed perpetual tears as an eternal flame to commemorate the story.

———

When I first moved to San Diego, I struggled to find a home. I was evicted after six weeks from the three hundred square foot apartment I had found online. My landlord had gone into foreclosure. I wrestled with road maps and one-way streets in a completely unfamiliar city as I searched for a new apartment. Many times I liked what I saw and would check requirements off the list. Picturing my sparse furnishings in this new home, I'd get excited about the possibilities. But just as it seemed that a deal could be struck, I would casually mention my dog, India, and my sales pitch threaded with my best Southern charm was met with a dead phone line, or the lease I clutched in my hands was immediately removed by the anxious fingers of a landlord-to-be.

So my search continued. And then I stumbled onto the perfect place. It was a small guesthouse with a fenced yard and a landlord who used to be a baker. As I once more casually mentioned my fuzzy roommate, I observed the all-too-familiar hesitation. But, unlike the others, she was willing to meet India, and then, though perhaps not enthusiastically, she agreed to give us a try.

I moved everything in and quickly made it a home. At the end of each workday, I looked forward to this special place of solace in a city with glaring spaces I felt inadequate to fill. One unforgettable day, I came home to find my dog proudly sitting next to a huge hole she had very conspicuously created in the center of the yard. In fact, it was more of a large pit than a hole. There was a huge pile of dirt covering the space where lush green grass had been visible. The well-manicured lawn my landlord spent weekends tending was now an eyesore. I was shocked that India would do such a thing and envisioned our immediate eviction.

My landlord acted with remarkable grace as I profusely apologized, and when I came home the next day, the hole had been neatly filled in and smoothed over. I was relieved; my guilt was assuaged.

But a few days later, India emptied the hole again. The massive, offensive pit was back. We repeated this cycle of apology, repair, and further destruction several times before resigning ourselves to the fact that the hole was there to stay. Still, my landlord demonstrated remarkable patience.

Months later, I returned home after a few weeks overseas. Dragging a worn suitcase, I stepped inside my familiar surroundings. Immediately, I went to the yard to greet India. When I stepped outside, my eyes widened incredulously at what I saw. My mouth curved into a slow, wonder-filled smile. Where the gaping eyesore once dwelled stood a beautiful tree that was positively spectacular. It was crooked in all the right places. The yard now looked like a scene from a storybook. I went to find my landlord, who grinned and quipped, "It seemed like the perfect place for a tree, don't you think?"

Yes, it was the perfect place, but until the tree had been planted, I had never noticed that anything was missing. The answer was not to cover up the hole. The solution was not to pretend the hole wasn't there. And it wasn't to leave the gaping chasm glaring back at us.

In this case, the answer was to give it purpose.

flawed pearls

Grief is a strange thing in that its memory is more characterized by what the relationship was or was not in life than by what characterized the death. For one kind, you look forward and ache over what has now been lost for the future. In an altogether different form, there is a grief that changes your perspective as you look backward and grieve what never truly was and can now never be.

The award-winning author Paulo Coelho is a beautiful writer, and his lines of pure poetry are disguised as novels. His book *The Witch of Portobello*, a mystical story with many unusual turns, remains on my shelf, no matter where I live. I often pull it off, brush my hand across the cover, and flip it open to a page I have nearly memorized.

The story begins in Beirut, Lebanon, a country that boasts of warm hospitality, platefuls of hummus and tabouli, the Mediterranean coast, and beautiful cedars. Known for their beauty, strength, and scent, the cedars of Lebanon are mentioned in poetry as a symbol of resilience and several times in the Old Testament with reference to their grandness and fortitude. It is said that with the onset of a first snowfall, cedars will turn their branches to rise toward the heavens. By assuming this new shape, they sustain the immense weight of snow and will not be crushed.

Coelho describes his heroine, Athena, as an unusual girl who possessed a sense of spirituality from the time of her youth. She married when she was nineteen and wanted to have a baby right away. Her husband left her when the baby was still young, and Athena had to raise him alone.

During one Sunday Mass, the priest watched as Athena walked toward him to receive Communion, and his heart was filled with dread.

She stood in front of the priest, drew her eyes closed, and opened her mouth to receive the bread. I picture her standing there in vulnerability, asking and wanting to receive what represents Christ's body, given for her. She was hungry for the grace that it offered.

But he did not give it to her.

The young girl opened her eyes, terribly confused. The priest tried to tell her in hushed tones that they would talk about it later, but she would not be turned away. She persisted until she received an answer.

"Athena, the Church forbids divorced people from receiving the sacrament. You signed your divorce papers this week. We'll talk later."[10]

She was crushed, speechless, numb. People began to step around her in line to receive the bread that was theirs. In an awful combination of seeing her as invisible and visible, they stepped around her, so she knew they knew she was there. But they bypassed her, for she was an obstacle in the way of their path to greater spirituality.

I imagine her to be devastated. She had lost something that mattered to her, something she thought would always be hers —

something she had given herself to. And when it was gone, it claimed her dreams, her respect, her ability to hope, and her very sense of self. She was alone, very alone. The book doesn't tell us if her family was able to help her, and I wonder if this was intentional. For there are some losses that leave us unmistakably and entirely alone, even when there are the few who are willing to stand in the center of the bull's-eye with us. What was lost was actually something that was part of us. It may heal in time, I suppose, but it will never grow back as it was. We talk of phantom pain associated with missing limbs, and when a piece of our heart goes missing, I think a phantom pain remains in its stead too.

I imagine many of Athena's friends turned against her. Some saw her as tainted, regardless of the details. Perhaps others behaved as if she carried a contagious disease, warning her married friends to keep their distance lest they catch the bug of divorce. The most painful thing in her life, or the limited version they knew of it, was fodder for insensitive gossip and irreverent dinner-table conversation. Did they feel the severity of her pain? Did they have to watch when her body was racked with sobs, and tears burned her eyes and stained them red?

I imagine that her marital status became part of her name, as in "Athena, the girl who is divorced." I wonder if they told her there was no place for her in ministry, if they sat in comfortable chairs, dressed in their suits, and held meetings behind closed doors to decide, while their own stories remained tucked away with their coordinated handkerchiefs. Did someone say, "Do you know that God hates divorce?" And did she answer, "I know. So do I. Possibly even more than you"? I wonder if it hurt when they pinned the Scarlet *D* on her, or if she was so wounded and fragile she invited and fully accepted the pain and guilt to add to the punishment and shame she had inflicted on herself.

Did they know how hard it was for her to come to church that day? And now, in a final act of driving the knife into her gaping wound and out the other side, she was told she was no longer worthy to come to Christ, the one who could give refuge in her anguish. For unlike them, he *did* know all that lay within her heart. And it was to *him* that she actually answered, not the masses who tried to occupy his place.

As the priest finished administering the sacrament, he slowly stepped back to the altar. Athena stood in the same place where he left her and cried out what many have only cried on the inside: "A curse on all those who never listened to the words of Christ and who have transformed his message into a stone building. For Christ said: 'Come unto me all ye that labor and are heavy laden, and I will give you rest.' Well, I'm heavy laden, and they won't let me come to him. Today I've learned that the Church has changed those words to read: 'Come unto me all ye who follow our rules, and let the heavy laden go hang!'"[11]

Athena vowed to never set foot in a church again, and she turned on her heels and left with her crying baby, tears streaming down her own cheeks.

The priest could not forget her face, the forlorn look in her eyes, or the poignancy of her words. He had been faced with a philosophical dilemma, and he had chosen to show respect for the institution rather than the words on which that institution stood.

Years pass within the single chapter, and as he looks back on life and ministry, the priest affirms his confidence in God and in a practice of faith that is made up of human beings that he truly believed were trying to do the best they could, though they might fall short. But he said that he often thought back to that poor girl, for as time passed he grew to believe that it would only one day reveal the ultimate importance of Christ's words when he said, "Come unto me all ye that labor and are heavy laden, and I will give you rest."

Coelho's chapter ends with the priest's words: "I like to imagine that, when she left the church, Athena met Jesus. Weeping and confused, she would have thrown herself into his arms, asking him to explain why she was being excluded.... And looking at Athena, Jesus might have replied: 'My child, I've been excluded too. It's a very long time since they've allowed me in there.' "[12]

As for me, I imagine that Jesus took her broken heart and held it carefully, gently, in the palm of his hand.

I imagine he called her by her first name, and it was not followed by middle names of all of her failures. I imagine he loosened the Scarlet *D* they had pinned to her and told her the letter she carried was his image and his name.

I imagine she threw herself at his feet and said, "This is who I am." He would have opened his hand to show her the scar of a nail. Maybe he pointed to the mark that the spear had left in his side. And he called her to his table and told her that his broken body was also offered for her.

And I imagine that she left with a grace all-sufficient for *her* broken story too.

⎯⎯

An uplifting rhythm of friendship that is unusual for two women became a unique bond among four. We had our moments that were not seamless, perhaps when one met with lack of enthusiasm from the panel for a new boyfriend or when we took turns retreating from life into a place of inner angst and needed to be sought out. We were girls. It was not always simple.

We dotted the country with vacations and birthday celebrations, laughed with each other until we cried, and cried —

surrounded by each other — until we laughed again. We developed a coded system, an SOS of sorts, that was called on to discuss things like the "mean and ridiculous" file created from unduly harsh criticism e-mailed to a writer, or to vent a frustration that took any one of us to the edge. And with a flurry of short e-mails, each of us eyed the office clock until quitting time, shut down any other demands, and trickled in to the same undisclosed location. An in-depth analysis from simultaneously offered opinions meant closure to the "mean and ridiculous" because it simply couldn't stand up to the force of four. On those occasions, it wasn't about bringing someone back from the edge; it was about the confidence there was in the unrelenting arm strength of Red Rover on the other side of it.

One summer week in June, a member of our brigade was traveling in Thailand. She had tasted succulent mango with sticky rice, sipped sweetened Thai iced coffee, and meandered through the river in a longboat. On her last day, she was still searching for the perfect gift for each of her friends back home — for individual gifts that fit each person, because obviously the same thing couldn't speak to all.

She had her nose up to the jewelry case in the cottage emporium marketplace, admiring yellow topaz and reddish-brown tiger's eye gems. She lowered her eyes to the bottom shelf to look at rows of flawless pearls, Dippin' Dots of snow white and vanilla. There were shades of soft pink and rose that looked like something Jackie O would have paired with a pillbox hat and a cap sleeve summer dress to grace the cover of *Vogue* magazine.

Each pearl was shaped with rounded contours. Then her eyes caught the anomaly of an oddly shaped gemstone. It was unevenly shaped rather than a perfect sphere. Even the color was different, striking in its contrast as the light reflected on its silvery midnight hue. She looked up and caught the attention of the petite woman standing behind the counter, her straight black hair gathered into a ponytail that hung down her back.

The salesperson reached a dainty hand behind the glass and retrieved the small box of four similar gems. As my friend clasped one between her fingers, she could feel the uneven ridges that she could see with the magnifying glass of her eye. She glanced back at the rows of perfection behind the glass, but the irregular beauty of this one drew her to its detail.

These were black pearls, the woman explained. They did not fit the proper parameters, the right category of proportion and texture. Because of this, they were deemed imperfect and were considered less valuable.

Lifting one between her fingers, the woman angled her head to study it. "Some people see them as flawed," she said as the light caught an uneven angle and revealed a depth of silvery glitter, "while others see them as special." She placed the pearl back inside its case and closed her lips into a smile. With a nod of her head she walked away to allow my friend to decide which side of the case she stood on.

She purchased all four.

———

I was thirty-one years old. I was half Asian and an American citizen. I was single.

There are many other things that describe my life, that tell you who I am, but I had not gotten further than that in recent conversations. I had developed a growing interest in the eventual possibility of adopting a child and decided to do some initial research to better understand the process in preparation for any future decisions.

I was actually there just to visit the children's home, but when they mentioned they administered adoptions, I casually said I was interested in exploring the possibility one day — and suddenly I found myself sitting across the table from Sister Maria, the decision maker in charge of adoption for this home located in a developing country.

She asked where I was from.

"Are you in school?" she asked, her hands carefully folded on the table in front of her.

"No, I graduated from college about ten years ago," I answered, feeling a tinge of excitement.

"Are you married?"

"No," I replied. Before I could continue, she laughed — a full-bodied, intentional laugh.

"Then why are you here?" she asked. "If you are not married, you have nothing to offer a child," she declared with an authoritative finality that concluded my interview.

Her words stung. I was hurt, but I was also somewhat incredulous. I was in a country that is said to have more than thirty-five million orphaned children, approximately the population of the state of California. This home had several rooms filled with little ones under the age of five. Dedicated volunteer workers moved quickly to keep up with cries, falls, and mealtimes. Make no mistake, this home loved these children, and they were safe and off the streets. But it is still an institution, and the number of children is vastly larger than the number of caregivers. The resources are limited, and no child belongs to anyone in particular. The children were not wearing diapers, and many of the toddlers walked with an uneven childlike gait, their shorts visibly wet from urine. Was this so much better than belonging to me?

She continued with her friendly chatter and then closed our

meeting by saying, "And please pray for us. We have so many children here with no homes, and nobody wants them." The irony was startling. Here I was, willing and able to bring a child into my life. I stood in front of her with my arms empty, looking at the children about whom she was speaking — all of whom needed to be held.

I felt small and embarrassed as I left.

Later that day, I weaved my way through one of the most densely populated cities in Asia, crowded with pedestrians, taxicabs, and rickshaws, while a layered sound track of bustling life accompanied the motions. Amidst the chaos, I looked down to see an eight-year-old boy walking beside me and grinning. He held a pole of colored scarves. I shook my head uncertainly to indicate that I didn't want one, but I felt badly that I didn't. He kept walking with me, asking my name and where I was from. We found ourselves walking through an outdoor market, with people and stands strategically arranged like a game of Tetris. We wandered around, and he patiently sat on the step with his hands in his chin while I looked at some jewelry. As I stepped out of the stall, he grinned and resumed his place as we wandered some more.

"Would you buy me some milk?" he asked. I was a little surprised, as I had never been asked this. I said, "Yes, I will certainly buy you milk." He took my hand and led me in a direction he seemed familiar with. Moments later, he stood with a smile on his face, clutching a large box of protein powder that would make several glasses of "milk." His only question was whether or not there was a prize hidden in that particular box. "No, there is not," the man behind the counter said. My little friend shrugged his shoulders, and the smile returned. He walked with me for a

while longer and then said he needed to go. He curled his forefinger to ask me to lean closer.

As I leaned down to his eye level, he smiled and said softly,
"I thank God I saw you today." And with that, he disappeared
into the crowd.

I echoed the same sentiments to his disappearing shadow. In
him, I saw something I was missing. In me, he found something
the woman with folded hands at the table had perhaps failed to
see.

Oddly enough, he did not ask my age, my ethnic background,
or my marital status. We didn't get that far, for he measured me
by an altogether different standard.

⸻

I had strung the black pearl my friend gave me on a simple chain
around my neck. Whenever I wear it, I remember the priceless
gift she gave by what she chose to see in me, and how I want
to view others whose lives do not fit within our parameters of
acceptable.

Some see them as flawed. I want to see them as special.

chapter 12

recognizing beauty

They invited me into their house, and I folded my hands in greeting to each one. Their skin stretched across their bodies unevenly; the scarring on their faces, necks, and arms revealed past traumas. But it was always the sparkle in their eyes and the genuine warmth in their smiles that I was unable to look past.

They were victims of bride burning. Someone had doused them in kerosene, struck a match, and set them on fire. But these weren't the merciless acts of strangers. These deeds were carried out by husbands or mothers-in-law. They would have known what was coming; they would have tried to scramble away. They would have cried out in pain as the flames melted their skin, cries that would bring some of their children running to try to rescue their mothers. A young girl sat next to her mother now, her face bearing the scars of the love that walks through fire to save another.

Thousands of people, mostly women, are victims of burnings each year in India. Some inflict it on themselves in attempted suicides or in desperate cries for help. Some are reported as accidents. Many are the result of unpaid or insufficient dowries. Conservative figures estimate that twenty-five thousand young brides in India alone are set on fire each year.

I was in Bangalore, India, visiting a project that provides aftercare, surgical treatment, physical therapy, and microfinance opportunities for burn victims. It was not my first visit, but it was the first time I was meeting Prema. Her reputation had preceded her, and I felt honored to be sitting across from her at the table.

A young girl walked into the room, and I stood up to say hello. She was a burn victim who had previously received treatment. When I first met her a year ago, she was ever so carefully embroidering delicate reams of strawberry-red fabric. I had commented on how beautiful it was, and she had blushed and smiled. Only months later, I opened a delivered package to uncover a beautiful embroidered sari of strawberry red.

A staff member stepped into the room and called to Prema. They were ready for her. She explained that she needed to examine a patient and asked if I wanted to accompany her. I nodded and followed her into a small examining room sectioned off with white curtains. When I drew back the curtain, I was not mentally prepared for what I would see. I swallowed hard and refused to let an audible sound escape from my lips.

I had never looked upon such physical pain. The patient was sitting on the side of a cot with his arms outstretched. From his waist up to his neck was exposed, raw flesh. His arms were extended because he could not lay them by his side. It was not easy to look at, not because it wasn't pretty, but because it screamed of sheer agony. He looked right at me as he measured his breathing in a calculated attempt to handle the pain. It seemed as though he was waiting to see if I would take one look at him and turn around in horror. There was no way I was going to disrespect him by bearing witness to what he endured and then rejecting the sight of his wounds as if it were me that had to endure the pain. So I met his eyes and consciously took a step toward him.

I could see patches of pink flesh, but most of his upper body was covered in a white film of what I assumed was ointment. But when Prema carefully laid a strip of cloth directly on his raw flesh, she turned to me and explained that it was pus from infection. Before she could treat him, she needed to remove the pus, because if she bandaged over it, she would trap the infection inside. She called out to the nurse for help and demonstrated how to carefully peel back the gauze, thus removing the pus as it adhered to the cloth strip. The young man began to shudder, and as they peeled away each strip, he let out a wail his bravery could not contain.

"How old is he?" I asked.

She repeated the question to him in Tamil. "Twenty-six," she answered as she continued to work.

I was standing next to him now, feeling completely helpless to alleviate his suffering. He stared straight into my eyes, and I was afraid to move for fear that a human presence in his line of vision may be providing a focal point as he was rocked by waves of pain, like combating motion sickness by finding a stationary point to trick the mind into believing you are, in fact, grounded.

I would not have taken his hand to extend comfort because it was not culturally appropriate. But I was keenly aware that this was not even an option. He would not have been able to receive and endure a common gesture of support, for his hands were wounded as well. Beyond even the obvious agony, I considered how lonely it would feel to be unable to receive the human touch. I am an affectionate person; pictures from childhood show me safely wrapped around my mother's leg, and if I could get away with it, I would probably still do that to friends and family. I couldn't imagine the loneliness of a lack of human connection — not because no one was offering it, but because you couldn't endure it.

"He tried to commit suicide," she explained.

English was not his first language, but I could tell he understood what was being said. He continued to look at me and then slowly parted his lips and uttered, "I don't know why ..." in my language. His brown eyes were deep, yet empty — empty of any emotion other than physical anguish. But it spoke of something else, seeming to reveal that something, even perhaps hopelessness, had been there at one time but had exhausted itself into darkness.

Another deep breath, another cry, as another strip of gauze was removed.

"When did this happen?" I asked. Again Prema spoke to him in Tamil. She momentarily stopped what she was doing to look up at me as she relayed his answer. "Two months ago."

Here I was unable to stifle a reaction. How had he moved or slept? How had he even survived for two months in this kind of physical torture? The government hospital had turned him away repeatedly because their beds were full. He had nowhere to go until he heard about this clinic.

I met his eyes again and wondered what had happened in his life that made him want to die. Not just that. I wondered what compelled him to want to punish himself so severely even in that death. I thought it was a miracle that he had survived like this for two months, and I wondered what "why" he had found deep within his soul that prevailed in spite of a conclusion that he no longer wanted to do so. Whatever it was, I prayed to God that it would rise up in him, that somewhere he had someone or something he knew was waiting for him — someone or something to help him endure the "how."

As the nurses worked together, I followed Prema back to her office. Unopened cans of Coke and Orange Fanta sat on a tray next to empty glasses and a bowl of potato chips. I didn't make an attempt to reach for anything. The face of despair I had just seen stifled hunger.

"Will you be able to help him?" I asked as I pointed back toward the white curtains.

"Yes," she replied. "He has good skin on his legs. When the infection clears, he will go in for surgery."

The fire had not claimed more than 60 percent of his body, and so he would survive. She explained that in the United States, even if a body is completely covered with third-degree burns, there is a possibility for treatment. But in India, if burns claimed over 60 percent of the body, there was nothing they could do. There wasn't enough skin to graft, and there wasn't enough skin available through a donor bank.

"When you say there is nothing you can do …" I trailed off before asking the question.

"They will likely die," she said quietly.

I looked up at her face, a face that reflected hope in the midst of much suffering. I think my face still mirrored the suffering man's doubt and had not yet transitioned to the hope before me now. Which was ironic, because although I couldn't fathom his pain, *she* could. She had once felt that burn on her skin.

When she was eight years old, Prema returned home from school and tried to light a burner of the stove to make some tea. But something went wrong, and the stove erupted into flames. The skin of her face literally melted into her neck, and 50 percent of her body was wounded by burns. She was rushed to Christian Medical College Hospital for treatment.

As her mother, Rosie, watched her daughter suffering in agony and battling for her very life, she made a plea to God. *Save my child, and I will dedicate her to your service. One day she will return to this hospital and be your hands.*

Young Prema cried because of her pain. She cried because she didn't want the doctors to touch her painful wounds. She cried because she had lost her hair. In an effort to soothe her, the doctor told her that if she would allow him to treat her, he would give her his hair if he could. This calmed her sobs to a whimper and slowly she settled down and allowed them to treat her. She laughs now when she recalls the sincere offer extended to her by the doctor, who was, in fact, bald.

After six months in the hospital, Prema returned home. Her parents had removed all the mirrors from the house, and so although she saw reactions of horror from strangers who passed by on the street, she had not seen her own face. After one year, she inadvertently walked past a mirror. Looking at a scarred face she did not recognize, she cried out in anger, in terror, in devastation. With the wisdom of a mother, Rosie first let her daughter cry. And when it had been enough, she looked into her daughter's tear-filled eyes and spoke to the truth that was both reality and potential. "This is your face now, and you will have to live with it. No one can change that. But what you do with your life is in your hands, and only you can determine that."

Over the next six years, Prema endured fourteen surgeries before deciding she had had enough. It was time to focus on other things. And in 1980, fifteen years after the day of her accident, she returned to the same hospital — but this time not as a patient. She had obtained her medical degree and was accepted into a residency position, working under the very same doctor who had treated her and offered her hair he wished he had been able to give to her.

Prema specialized in plastic and reconstructive surgery and became a surgeon. Today, she is the head of the Department of Plastic and Reconstructive Surgery at Christian Medical College Hospital. She has been the recipient of many awards, including the "Triumph of Human Spirit Award" from the Rotary Club of Chennai. She has traveled around the world and has not only trained Ethiopia's first plastic surgeon but is now setting up the first burn care unit there. In India, she launched Agni Raksha, the project I now witnessed.

She is grateful for her life, for her gifted hands. Her dreams have all been fulfilled, except for one. "I should have a quick death, and when people see me, they should say, 'She looks so beautiful and peaceful.' I want to look more beautiful than I am now when I meet my Lord." But here she has asked for the impossible, for no miracle can work against itself and actually reduce what already is.

Margaret Mitchell, the famous Southern author who claimed a Pulitzer Prize for her epic novel *Gone With the Wind*, once said, " I was never one to patiently pick up broken fragments and glue them together again and tell myself that the mended whole was as good as new. What is broken is broken — and I'd rather remember it as it was at its best than mend it and see the broken places as long as I lived." When I hear Prema tell her story, I can't help but disagree with Ms. Mitchell.

As Prema sat across from me in a striking sari of pink and green, I was captivated by her. She exuded strength, not of brute force, but something reminiscent of the architectural genius and grace of a pillar.

She is a strikingly beautiful woman. It is not in spite of the scars, and it is not only because of them. A scar is not the source of beauty; it can only indicate the presence of something that lies beneath its surface and guide you to its hidden depths. And in doing so, it becomes the symbol of beauty itself.

The beauty of her spirit is genuinely enhanced by the presence of the scars because they speak of a story. If by some miracle she could erase the scars today, I would ask her not to, because they would take away from a face and an aura that told me I was in the presence of something exquisite.

Several months back, while in Phnom Penh, Cambodia, I stood in the middle of what is called "the killing fields," open fields that contain mass graves. It was silent and still. The smell of incense wafted from a small memorial nearby. Torn clothing protruded from the ground, and I looked down at a swatch of soiled gray fabric that might have been the sleeve of a shirt or a piece of pant leg. Claiming Communist ideals, Pol Pot led his regime to imprison, torture, and kill the educational and professional leaders of the society it sought to control. Somewhere buried under the earth was a man who was father to an eight-year-old daughter at the time of his death. Her name was Channary, and as I stood next to her, we took gentle steps, aware that every place we trod was on ground that loosely covered the memory of a life.

Channary began to speak of her experience as a child sentenced to a labor camp. While forced to do manual labor, she cut her toe against a rock one day. The toe became infected, and because she received no treatment, it healed in crooked form. She pointed down to it as it peeked out from her sandal. "I've always thought it was so ugly. I hated that toe," she said as she shook her head. Her frown seamlessly turned into a soft smile as she concluded. "My husband says it's his favorite one. It reminds him of what I came through."

———

I saw the movie *Slumdog Millionaire* five times in the theater. I loved the layers to the film, the juxtaposition of beauty and tragedy that mirrors the real tension that exists in living. A British film that was set in Mumbai, it became an entertainment blockbuster that went on to claim eight Oscars at Hollywood's Academy Awards and four Golden Globe Awards.

It is the story of Jamal, a boy who survived childhood in the slums and ended up as the unlikely contestant on the Indian version of *Who Wants to Be a Millionaire?* The film explores the idea of destiny — whether we create it or simply live out what is already determined for us. In an intermingling of Eastern and Western philosophy, we feel the tension between a past that Jamal cannot change and his being empowered to shape his future. Jamal believes it is his destiny to find Latika, the girl he loves, whose own past is characterized by tragedy — she had become the possession of a drug lord.

By the end of the story, Jamal gets his girl, but it is not without a fight. In the final scene, as they meet, he walks slowly toward Latika. He gently lifts a covering off her head to look at her face. He studies her features and is drawn to her left cheek, where a deep scar marks an otherwise flawless face.

As he takes her face in his hands, it is the scar to which he first draws his lips. When he does this, the picture flashes in reverse before our eyes, back to the moment the injury occurred. The message is perfection. He acknowledges the scar and sees it as something to be handled carefully. He does not pretend it isn't there; he does not try to erase its presence, for that would only take away from who she was.

With an element of poetry, the kiss speaks to a love that could turn back time, as it were, and heal the very moment of injury itself.

———

The truth is, scars are an important part of our stories, as they are to Prema, to Channary, and to Latika in *Slumdog Millionaire*. A scar can remain as a tribute to what happened; it tells us something went wrong, that someone got hurt. A scar lets us know that she survived. The tension between flawed and special reveals something about the viewer too. It weeds out those who only appreciate the kind of beauty that is obvious. And it affords the opportunity to those with true character to explore beneath the rough edges to uncover an altogether different kind of beauty. But it's the kind you have to roll up your sleeves to discover.

Then again, if it were not so, it wouldn't be *special*.

chapter 13

heroic limitations

When *Grimm's Fairy Tales* was first published in 1812, the book created much controversy, as readers felt some of the material was not suitable for children. The second and third editions reflected significant edits in response to the concerns. Thus, the evil mothers in "Hansel and Gretel" and "Snow White" were changed to evil stepmothers (because apparently this wouldn't have a negative effect on children and familial relationships). Notably, "Rapunzel" was edited to include a wedding. Originally, the seemingly naive heroine of this story commented to the evil fairy about the tightening threads of her dress around her growing belly. The fairy is furious, for Rapunzel was pregnant, revealing that the prince's visits to the tower were not entirely innocent. The later publication rewrote the story to have the prince marrying Rapunzel (albeit in an unofficial ceremony) while she is in the tower. The pregnancy was not mentioned until the end of the story, when Rapunzel wandered the wilderness with her twins.

I find it interesting that over time we seem to have moved further and further away from any disturbing elements in our stories to the tales of today, where pain is minimal and temporary. Certainly what is appropriate must be considered, but have *all* of the edits been implemented for the sake of what is appropriate for children? Or is the broadening swipe of the eraser on reality to protect ideals that we as adults long to cling to — our view of what we believe life *should* be? And in the real world, when we cannot use an eraser or press fast-forward, it is a tortuous challenge to recognize when we can intervene, when circumstances are beyond our power to right a clear wrong, and how to live with the haunting questions and lasting impact of both.

I was supposed to follow the people in front of me, a simple but nearly impossible task. I stepped over goats and sleeping dogs and tried to weave my way through the crowd of people. I needed to look down to make sure I wasn't stepping on or in something. I needed to look up to make sure a motorcycle or taxi speeding its way down the congested pathway wasn't about to hit me. The mission of all drivers was to get to their destination, while the mission of every pedestrian was to not get in their way. For if the driver was confronted with the choice, the destination would prevail.

I was back in Kamathipura, the red-light district in Mumbai and the largest of its kind in Asia. I was there to visit again Devaraj and his organization, Bombay Teen Challenge. He was leading the way, and I was doing my best to follow, though my senses were overloaded.

Beads of sweat remained along my brow and trickled consistently down my back. I twirled my hair and secured it with a clip to allow my neck to breathe. The streets were packed as usual, and children were running around in bare feet for a game of pickup cricket among the crowds.

Brothels line the unpaved roads, one after another after another. Time and heat have chipped away at the shades of light green, yellow, or orange paint on concrete buildings of various heights. The first time I was there, seventy thousand women were somewhere inside. Black bars line the windows, and as we walked by, I saw the whites of dark eyes looking back.

I asked Devaraj why some women are allowed to stand out on the street and others remain behind the bars. "When they stop trying to escape, they are allowed on the street," he answered. I have never really been able to decide what makes me sadder — the ones trapped behind bars or the ones who don't need the bars anymore because they have given up.

We crossed the street to meet up with our group at the clinic. We stood talking outside the doorway, discussing HIV antiretroviral medications and costs, the health status of twenty women we supported for treatment, and the nutrition they were given each day for comprehensive care.

We were interrupted midsentence with an ominous popping sound and the commotion of people scattering. In seconds there was an explosion, and we backed into the clinic, shielding our faces with our arms. A man had been sitting on the ground next door with a small gas stove, probably making a nice lunch for himself. The stove exploded, leaving shrapnel scattered and everyone startled, but no one seemed to be hurt.

As we made our way down the street, Devaraj stopped to warmly greet familiar faces. They all looked up at him and beamed at the kind words and respect he offered. He once told me that it took two years of trying to speak to the women, to tell them they were there to help, before the first woman would acknowledge him. Life had taught them to distrust, especially a man, and he had to be patient and consistent to alleviate their understandable suspicions. He persisted for two years and has remained for twenty.

I stopped instantly when I heard a piercing scream. I looked up in the direction of a third-story window in front of me. A crowd had gathered below on the street, pointing up to a woman outside the window. She was trying to jump, but two men were combating her attempt to flee, grabbing at a leg or flailing arm to pull her back inside the brothel room. She was screaming in protest and trying desperately to resist them. Their strength was greater, and her screams were silenced as they pulled her back inside and secured the window.

The crowd dispersed, and everyone continued on their way. I was stunned and stared up at the closed window. She may not have died had she jumped, but she must have thought she would have. And that must have seemed better than the alternative in that room. I looked at Devaraj, and he returned my silent anguish and quickly guided me through the crowd to the car that would take me away while he remained.

When I returned home, I recounted the story to a girlfriend. The screams of a girl held against her will haunted me. My friend was incensed. "How could you leave?" she asked. "If I had been there, I would have gone into that brothel to get her."

I was silent, because I felt painfully guilty that I had been utterly helpless in the situation. My head knew that in that context I could not just march into a brothel armed with justice and be the hero. There were many possible outcomes, but walking out with a girl set free is not one of them.

If I stormed a brothel, I would be dealing with a system that has a dark underworld. Over time, I could potentially build a relationship with a brothel madam and buy freedom for a girl. This is a complicated solution that could perpetuate the system that sells human beings and may lead to encouraging traffickers by contributing to their financial gain and refueling a system that will buy another victim.

I was limited by a world that was much bigger than me and discovering that my limitations were downright painful.

I do not know what happened to her. I don't know if she tried to jump again. I don't know if she was ever successful in leaving. I hate that I do not know any of these answers, and I hate that I could not fix her horrifically unjust world that day.

⁓

Two years had passed since that day now etched in my memory. I was back along the familiar road in Kamathipura, the haunting picture playing in my mind as it did every time I returned to the place where it happened. I walked into the HIV clinic I had planned to visit, greeted the doctor, and sat down in a chair he pulled out for me.

A few minutes later, one of the staff members walked in, holding the hand of a little girl. She sat across from me, next to Devaraj, who welcomed her affectionately. She curled up against him, obviously knowing she could find safety by his side. She sat in her chair, swinging her legs underneath her. Her hair was in pigtails, and she was dressed in orange capri pants and an orange and white striped T-shirt.

Her name was Mary, and she was about six years old. She lived in a brothel with her mother, but her mother had disappeared, and Mary was now there on her own. The brothel madam phoned Bombay Teen Challenge. Following protocol, they launched an official investigation into the whereabouts of Mary's mother before they could gain legal custody. If they did not do this and instead removed Mary without possessing the proper documentation that she had been abandoned and was a minor, they could find themselves in serious legal trouble. If they neglected to do this, Mary's mother — if she was in fact alive and one day returned — the brothel or law enforcement could have grounds to issue a legal complaint. While the investigation was under way, they visited her regularly to monitor her protection as best they could.

Mary stayed in the clinic with us for a little while, making silly faces and giggling in amusement. Eventually someone took Mary by the hand and led her back to the brothel that was still her home. We concluded our meeting in the clinic and walked out into the story-filled streets.

I stopped instantly when somehow, through the clamor of cars and busyness, I heard a persistent calling. I looked up and scanned the dilapidated building in front of me. My eyes landed on a third-story window where I saw movement. I squinted carefully and caught a glimpse of orange and white stripes. A little hand had slipped through the bars and was waving emphatically. The glare of white teeth told me she was smiling as she tried to catch our attention. I held up my hand rather weakly and waved back. I looked back pathetically to Devaraj, who nodded his head decidedly and reassuringly. "We're on it, I promise." And I knew I could believe him.

When I returned home, I wrote often to ask about her fate, pestering them to know what happened. I now had two pictures ingrained in my mind, and I could not compartmentalize the second one into a category of helpless.

Three weeks later, Devaraj sent me a picture of Mary in her new home, safely in their care. I have seen her each time I have returned. Her dark hair is trimmed into a cute pixie style; her eyes reflect boundless energy and excitement. On my last visit, she slapped the palms of my hands to play Miss Mary Mac, laughing uproariously when I playfully missed the triple slap.

I know what happened to her; I know she will be loved and taken care of. And I am relieved to know these answers. I am deeply grateful that someone was able to change Mary's unjust world into one that is good.

There are countless similar stories. None of them have a quick solution, and precious few have an easy solution. The ones that I cannot fix are at times too much to bear. But it is not a war I disengage from because I do not know what I can win. We have to continue to fight — for the individual and against evil and destructive forces — because the cause is always worthy.

And once you have stepped into this world, you can never walk away.

Once you have been made aware, you have a responsibility to care.

humanity that heals

Virginia and Fred have been married for fifty-four years. They have a beautiful family of children and grandchildren, and for some reason they have allowed me to feel as though I am a part of it. Virginia is one of the few people who have not forgotten the art of putting pen to paper. She writes me letters every month, asking how I am and where I am, and she is always concerned about my love life, or lack thereof. She always closes with the reminder of an open invitation to come for a visit with my dog. Virginia doesn't even like dogs.

I spent a long weekend with them one autumn in the beautiful mountains of Cashiers, North Carolina. We took India for long, leash-free walks over winding tree-lined paths. India exhausted herself each day running the mountain trails and diving into the lake for a swim and meeting us on the other side. Then the three of us sat in front of a cozy stone fireplace in the evenings, the dog quietly at our feet and each of us with a book in hand. We talked or didn't talk with equal ease and depth.

Hailing from New Orleans, Louisiana, Fred speaks with a wonderful Southern drawl that makes every word sound lovely. Virginia is from Bay St. Louis, Mississippi, the place they now make their home. They are the classic Southern couple. He is kind and speaks to me in a gentle voice that makes me feel like a little girl whose grandfather will buy her any ice cream flavor she chooses. Virginia is a wonderful combination of traits that embody a real woman. She is sensitive. She can be unapologetically vulnerable. She's got a bit of fireball in her too, the kind that lets you know she has fought her battles and knows who she is. There is no pretense; there is just someone very real. Whenever she sees me, she envelops my hand in both of hers, which is like sitting by the warmth of that fire.

An experienced and gifted architect, Fred built their dream home in Bay St. Louis in 1979, every detail and type of wood grain selected by his trained eye. It was the single setting their grandchildren knew for every Christmas tradition. On August 29, 2005, Hurricane Katrina roared through with 120-mile-per-hour winds and a 27-foot storm surge, making it the deadliest and costliest hurricane in United States history, with figures estimating that the economic impact for Mississippi and Louisiana would exceed 150 billion dollars.

Virginia and Fred escaped personally unharmed, but they saw their hometown forever changed. Beautiful manifestations of history and architectural design, as well as written records of libraries, were obliterated from the community. When the walls to their dream house collapsed, mementos like wedding pictures, baby photos, family heirlooms, jewelry, and extraordinary art had vanished.

About a week after the storm, their daughter Lisa went to the property. Fred had built the house with a concrete foundation and support beams that elevated the house above the ground. The house may have been destroyed, but the frame and foundation of his genius survived. Lisa surveyed the damage. Lowering herself onto what must have still been a soup of water, mud, and debris, Lisa crawled flat on her belly, using her elbows for mobility to venture inside the cave the resilient stilts had created underneath the shell of the former house. Using her hands as shovels, she plunged through the caked mud, looking for anything she might recover. It required unusual persistence, even an illogical stubbornness in what seemed to be a positively messy, if not reasonably impossible, task. But then she felt something at her determined fingertips. As she continued to scrape and dig, a treasure was revealed.

I asked her what made her go back. She shrugged and smiled softly. "I don't know," she said. "I felt so helpless. I didn't know what to do for them. I just thought I could at least try; maybe I would find something worth saving."

In 1955, Virginia had walked down the aisle, a bride ready to meet her groom. Dreams were fresh, and hope abounded. Her ivory dress was trimmed with patterns of delicate lace and cinched at her narrow waist before falling in soft lines to the floor. Around her neck she wore a single strand of off-white pearls, a gift Fred had given to her in celebration of this day that would stamp a permanent imprint on their lives.

When her wedding pearls were lost in the Katrina storm fifty years later, Virginia shed tears for this priceless gift a storm had claimed.

Propped on her belly amid the wreckage, Lisa fingered the strand of pearls in her soiled hands. Fully intact, not a single pearl was lost.

She went on to recover every individual fork, knife, and spoon from her grandparents' set of silverware. The time it must have taken and patience it must have required; the clothes she must have ruined; the dirt under her fingernails she must have accumulated. To an onlooker, it was a mass of debris dissolving in a muddy soup of quicksand, and a colossal waste of time. Anyone would have easily assumed that what was lost was lost. But sometimes, *sometimes*, it's not lost; it's just *missing*. And it takes an act of love — the act of someone willing to roll up her sleeves, get her hands dirty, and go on an archaeological dig — to find it.

———

Feeling a nagging itch to get away, a good friend called and asked if I would be interested in going with her to San Francisco for the weekend. I'm always up for spontaneous adventure, especially when it involves packing a bag. So after a few phone calls to juggle her master's degree classes and my upcoming travel commitments, we found the perfect two days to squeeze it in.

Perhaps we were just ready for a change of scenery, or perhaps it was the diverse culture of San Francisco, but we each quickly embarked on a new dating relationship with the city. As is always the case with the rose-colored glasses of infatuation, it was the perfect city. The streets made more sense; the coffee tasted better; the people were friendlier; and we even liked *ourselves* better in San Francisco. It didn't even matter when we found ourselves lost, far from our intended destination after trying to navigate multiple forms of public transportation. It didn't matter when the jazz club we prepared for by primping to raspy Louis Armstrong tunes didn't actually play jazz at all. We claimed the city as our own and turned a blind eye to its flaws. My friend sheepishly hid the oversized map we had to pull out more often than we cared to admit, but I suspect it was the Pollyanna glee and the exaggerated hanging off the sides of cable cars when gliding down hilly streets that gave us away as tourists.

After an afternoon of shopping, we made a reservation at a fantastic Italian restaurant based on the recommendation of a stranger. Slipping on our heels and tying up our hair, we set off for our night out. We walked outside into the perfect evening temperature and hailed a cab that dropped us off outside a quaint restaurant. We walked inside the French doors and into Tuscany. The obviously stressed and overworked manager somewhat gruffly led us to our table, although we immediately forgave his manner because, of course, it was San Francisco and therefore we didn't mind impatient people. After being seated at a small window table, we were greeted by our server. He was Italian, with dark eyes and a fantastic accent.

When dinner came to an end, he took my hand to say good-bye, brushing it with his lips, as it seems all Italian men should do. He smiled graciously and handed me a card with his name and phone number. "I would like to talk to you again sometime," he said, or something to that effect, I think. I smiled and tucked the card inside my wallet. I did not plan to call; I didn't even know him.

But I didn't throw the card away either. After some time had passed, and spurred on by the encouragement of a few friends, I nervously dialed the number — on a Saturday night, when I assumed he would be at work. I left a terribly awkward message, blurting out my full name, my city and state, and random information that stopped just short of my Social Security number. I am not a concise person, and this makes voice mail my great enemy. In my best respectable business voice, I finally brought my rambling message to an end by leaving my work phone number. Twice. In case he didn't catch it the first time, I guess. And miraculously, he called back.

"I didn't think I would hear from you," he greeted me.

"I didn't either," I admitted.

Several weeks later, I fidgeted uncomfortably in the baggage claim area of the San Diego airport, shifting my weight nervously from one red peep toe wedge heel to the other. Would I recognize him? What if he took one look at me and started climbing back up the escalator? I was reprimanding myself for having opened the weighted and foreboding door of the unknown, the possibility of disappointment, and any hint of rejection, even of friendship. To eliminate any chance of rejection in recent months, I had largely limited most of my interactions to my sister and my dog — two places where I can always count on finding love and never being turned away. But something small inside of me wanted to take this risk, to respond to this opportunity to meet someone who intrigued me. Thus far he was just a friend, but something about him seemed authentic, and I liked that.

I did recognize him, and he didn't run back up the escalator, though he might have wanted to. We headed over to Balboa Park, sat on the grass, and began to talk. There was an ease to his conversation and his friendship, and an honesty that was refreshing. He was open about his life, and the tragedies therein stirred depths in me. It was uncomfortable, because his story actually pained my soul, and it was comfortable, because it was a confrontation with humanity and its true spaces. He embraced life, explained life, and realized he couldn't possibly explain life. When he spoke about living, about people, about suffering, about love, about gnocchi, I wanted to pull out a notebook and write it all down. I knew I would never be able to remember the exact words, but I would never forget the impression or their artistic release.

We talked about the people close to us, and he said things like, "When you have hurt, you can hurt with them and tell them that you, too, have felt that burn on your skin." With every phrase, I found the English language blander and blander and wondered why we do not speak in such a way that transmits our thoughts into absorbed feeling and comprehension.

At a restaurant in Little Italy managed by an old friend of his, we filled our stomachs to excess with a dinner that included delightful presentations of polenta, lamb chops with mint sauce and risotto, pasta and homemade marinara, salmon and shrimp, an array of cheeses, crackers and grapes and creamy hazelnut gelato. With each course we progressively moved to new stages of a life journey. I found myself sharing some of the details I normally kept closely guarded because of the palpable fear that someone would discover their truths and look down on me. It had happened before, and I had grown so protective of my own story, my mistakes, and my raw hurt that at times I felt like a frightened, cornered animal ready to rear and pounce in order to protect myself. But I sensed he wouldn't judge me, and it was nothing short of utter relief. He was a troubled soul, his own tragedies deeply entrenched and lying there exposed. I knew he saw nothing simple about life, nothing admirable in something easy.

Setting down his knife and fork at one point, he folded his hands and said, "You see yourself in this very small way ... these horrible things ... because you are divorced?" I nodded, and as he put it into plain words, something about it didn't seem to fit in with the ultimate message of my faith, but I could not let the burden go either.

I felt physically pained to hear of all he had suffered — to picture him as a small child, then as a young person, then as an adult, and looking at him now, with the tragedies he carried with him, still visibly bleeding. In some ways it was overwhelming, but only because he looked each dark tragedy in the face, and he asked me to do the same, with his and with my own. Others mask or control their pains, keeping them contained in closed or time-released capsules. Instead, he was a bare canvas with unusual beauty portrayed — dark primary colors of raw affliction splattered in jarring brushstrokes that seemed heinous and yet could no longer be separated from the depth of the portrait itself. He had endured much and paid greatly for the poor choices of those who were supposed to love him most. And in his turmoil he had invited in further destruction and now struggled to escape its fierce stronghold.

The more we talked the more we silently acknowledged we were from two different worlds, existing on two planes that would never meet. But I felt I was in the presence of someone special, and I knew I would always consider him a friend I had spent years talking with. Or was it only hours?

Later that night, we sat in an eclectic coffee shop, one of my favorite spots in San Diego. We ordered lattes — steaming chai and hazelnut — the aroma a combination of cardamom and the nutty warmth that smelled like autumn turning into winter. We picked a corner table among the mismatched furniture and sat in comfortable silence for a few minutes, crunching homemade macaroons. We had an ongoing debate about love, about whether it could last for a lifetime. "Everything ends," he stated matter-of-factly. "Love is very simple, yet very complicated. It is the great key to unlock the door of life. But it is so heavy you cannot fit it into the lock. It is only one key, but it is so heavy you cannot hold on to it. All you can do is embrace the experience, the opportunity to love and be loved, and treasure it for as long as you have it before you."

Although I was a self-proclaimed love cynic, I could not resign myself to this. I said that if one does not think love has any chance of surviving, then I didn't understand how you could truly invest in it. Believing in the certainty of an end would become a self-fulfilling prophecy. It seemed like crossing the street. When I step off the curb, I know there is a chance I could get hit by a car. But it is the fact that I believe there is the chance I will cross safely that allows me to commit to the first step. If you told me a moving vehicle somewhere along the crosswalk would undoubtedly crush me, I would never take that step from the perceived safety of the edge of the sidewalk. "I *have* to believe," I stubbornly insisted, "that it can last." He grinned and chided, "Good luck." I laughed and acknowledged a touché by raising my coffee cup.

Then he looked at me intently, and his tone became quiet and serious. "I am so sorry for what happened to you," he began. "I am so sorry for how you hurt. You ... are angelic. I look at you and that is what I see — someone who should be protected." He studied my face and did not seem to be intimidated by my discomfort. He seemed to know it was not a discomfort of offense but one of shocking unfamiliarity. I fidgeted with the weight of the familiar chain around my neck. "I do not think you would be difficult to love. In fact, I think ... it would be the easiest thing in the world," he finished softly.

I could only stare back in utter speechlessness. For just like that, he handed me something I had misplaced years ago. Just like that, he handed back to me my self-respect. A heavy chain with the Scarlet *D* pendant loosened around my neck and, in what felt like slow motion, dropped to the floor.

For years, I had many a time tried to justify myself, my failure, my person, to so many others. Some were strangers who had limited insight into my life. Others were close and well-intentioned but somehow forgot the person in the midst of the black-and-white. They quoted verses of Scripture to tell me that this pointed to what I was. I remember words like *harlot*. They wrote letters to my father's ministry to share their opinions. They told me what I had done wrong, what I should have seen, how I could have avoided this anguish, how they would have done things differently. They pointed out how my situation affected my father's ministry, how all this must have devastated my parents. All of these were valid points.

Others had taken me out on dates and seemed to be in an argument with themselves about whether they could be with someone like me. Someone who was divorced. They wanted me to explain it to them, to their friends, to their parents when I shook hands as I met them at the family Thanksgiving dinner. I remember one telling me his friends had voted that it was OK to date me after he presented them with the full details of the story. He did not understand why this didn't please me, why I wasn't grateful for what was obviously sheer grace, and why I instead felt like a contestant on *Survivor* being voted on or off the island by people who really weren't entitled to know the full details of my qualifications.

Another would-be suitor said nothing, not a single word, when I told him. And I felt his palpable discomfort and silence if ever I referred to this part of my life. Still another did not bat an eye. He did not judge, that is true. And I must admit this was easier, though no less empty, than the reactions of outspoken judgment or deafening silence. In fact, he seemed to find it completely insignificant and never asked a single question. None of them walked away, but it was a different kind of sentence.

But never once in an abundance of conversations and exchanges had anyone looked at me and said, "I am sorry this happened, and it must have really, really hurt." The caring statement from my new friend was disarming, and I fought back tears that had been falling for a positively tiresome amount of time.

People say there are things in life that can't be explained or fully described, that you will just *know* when you see it and when you experience it.

They say that love is one of those things.

And now I know that grace is another.

When it was held open to me in pure form, it broke something that lived deep within, something unpredictable and raw that was seemingly fastened like a tumor to my heart, responding with an uprising when provoked or lying quietly in wait, but always present. Grace shattered the fastenings and transformed the fragments into something like freedom. And I experienced a faintly familiar and distant feeling of holding my head up, as though God himself was gently lifting my chin to look toward him. It was powerful. And it accomplished an infinitely greater transformation and restoration in me than the rebukes, the criticism, the indifference, and the loaded acceptance that seemed to sentence me to an eternity of being the lesser person.

I felt God reaching his healing hand into my heart, with all my imperfections and shortcomings, my failures and shattered dreams, and telling me that I was still his and was worthy of love. It was heart-wrenching. It was beautiful, and it made me want to believe in forgiveness, in love, in the power of human relationships, in the restorative strength of grace, in the ability to catch a glimpse of God on this earth.

I couldn't speak. I could only bite my lip as I felt the internal reconstruction at work in my spirit. My new friend seemed to know this, and he let it sit for a few moments to make sure it resonated. And then we pushed back our oversized coffee cups and headed for the door.

We said good night and made plans for breakfast in the morning before he returned home. But we never met for breakfast. I think we had already said good-bye, and we knew we wouldn't see each other again. We lived in different cities, facing logistics that were insurmountable because we resided in different worlds.

But he will never know what he gave me. I cried much throughout the night and the next day — and still, on occasion, now. I cry tears of sadness for him. I cry because of what he gave to me, and what he will never realize he gave to me.

He had misplaced the angel at the table that day. God sent Moses to free the enslaved Israelites, Rahab to save the lives of two spies far from home. And he sent another unlikely hero — a dark, wounded soul, with one foot in the abyss and one foot in celestial heights, to deliver grace and liberate me in divinely unorthodox fashion.

———

It was my first trip to South Africa. I had previously heard of its beauty, but no descriptions can do it justice. If you love mountains, it has some of the most beautiful slopes and skylines you've ever seen. If you love the beach, its white-tipped blue waters are breathtaking. It's a surfer's paradise, and whatever speaks to you in nature is there in exceptional form.

I was there with two colleagues and their three children. My first day began with intensity as I visited a shelter for abused women, a home for unwed mothers, a halfway house for women leaving prison, a home that cares for abandoned and abused children who are mentally challenged, and a rehabilitation home for women ensnared in drug addiction and prostitution.

I was at my final stop of the day in a completely unfamiliar part of town and with people I had never met before. I was listen-

ing to the story of a girl who had ended up on the street working for and abused by drug dealers. My host stepped out of the
room to take a phone call, and when she returned, she reported
that there was an emergency at home and she needed to leave
immediately.

"You'll be fine, right?" She asked it rhetorically, so I think
I nodded in reply. She asked the new friends we had just met if
they could help me get home. And with that, she had to go.

When I was finished, I called a colleague to see if someone
could come to get me. "Where are you?" he asked. I didn't really
know. "How far away are you?" Again, I didn't know. He didn't
hesitate and said, "OK, I'll be right there." Wherever "there" was.
The owner of the house didn't know the area he was coming
from, and he didn't know where the homeowner was located. But
we drove in his general direction and he in ours, and somehow
we miraculously found each other.

He greeted me with his typically friendly expression, tossed
me the keys, and said, "You're driving."

"But I've never driven here," I protested, "and it's a stick
shift." It was a different side of the road and different side of the
car than I was used to, and we were on curving lanes carved into
the side of a mountain. I knew how to drive a stick shift, but not
with my left hand.

"Ah, you'll be fine!" he said with a certainty I did not share.
"I have to speak in forty-five minutes, and I need to study my
notes." He needed to be somewhere else and had come to get me
without the slightest protest. I was going to *have* to drive.

I took the driver's seat, pulled my hair back into a ponytail — as if that would arm me to bypass every learned pattern —
and pulled back onto the road. I was very aware of oncoming
traffic on the side of the road I felt drawn toward and the fateful

drop-off along its edge. I overcompensated by hugging the side of the mountain.

"Careful; don't get too close to the inside," he cautioned as I did exactly that, crossing over the edge of the pavement with a thud and onto gravel that meant I was no longer on the road. "Or," he shrugged and grinned, "get as close as you'd like." He flipped to the next page.

Moments later, he looked up and said, "So how was your day?" I glanced at him but did not reply. I appreciated his attempts to be conversational, but at that moment I needed my full mental capacity to keep us alive. My eyes widened as I realized we were approaching a roundabout. What appeared to me to be an imminent death trap was perfectly unintimidating to my passenger — a Brit.

"Ummm ... what do I do now?" I asked with rising concern as I approached the circle.

"Go right," he instructed. And so I did exactly that. Occasionally I follow directions impeccably well. And that awoke him out of his previously unflustered temperament. "Noooo! Around the circle; then right!" He yelled as I swerved to avoid cars now facing us.

"Well, how was I supposed to know that?" My voice hit an uncharacteristically shrill octave as we screeched into a mad left turn and then a hard right around the circle.

"Because it's a roundabout," he said. "You *always* go left first!"

"We don't have these in Georgia," I said defensively, finally regaining control of the car and taking the right-after-the-left he intended.

He just shook his head and laughed, returning to his notes.

When we arrived at the house to meet his family, I breathed a sigh of relief. I was delighted I had not inflicted bodily harm on either one of us, and I gained quite the sense of accomplishment to know I could actually shift left-handed.

I was mentally fatigued but could not sleep that night. It wasn't so much the frightening drive that kept me awake, remembering just how close we were to the edge of the mountain. Rather, I had seen so much in one day that was harsh. And one image stood at the forefront of my mind and would not let me rest.

The room was filled with children. Each one was physically or mentally challenged, with varying levels of comprehension and mobility. This kind of experience was not easy for me, not because I felt uncomfortable, but because I felt useless. I didn't know how to best communicate, how to avoid underestimating their ability — potentially wounding their young spirit — or overestimating their resources and also wounding their spirit. I was afraid of hurting something that was already fragile. Unsure of myself, I bent down to greet a ten-month-old little girl who couldn't support her head. I tickled the bare foot of a little one lying on the ground. He smiled, but could not speak back.

In the far corner, I saw a boy who looked to be about eight years old. Two nylon straps secured him to an unpainted plywood board, and he was staring straight up at the ceiling. He had been dropped on his head when he was a baby, one of the caretakers told me. "Probably by a parent who had been drunk," she added, shaking her head as she walked away. The boy's neck was broken in the accident, leaving him paralyzed. Since then, he had been confined to lying flat on his back, strapped to a board without the ability to move his head, arms, or legs.

I wasn't sure how to communicate with him. I didn't know

if he knew I was there or if any words I spoke would resonate. I pulled my bag over my head, took it off, and laid it on the floor. Kneeling beside him, I didn't know what else to do, so I stroked his cheek in silence. His dark brown eyes didn't lose their focal point above, but his black eyelashes started to flutter, and slowly, soundlessly, tears began to roll down his cheeks.

Sometime later — I'm not even sure how long — my hosts told me it was time to go. I didn't want to leave, and it tore at my heart that I couldn't explain to the little boy that I had to leave. After several minutes I slowly took my hand away. His eyes moved for the first time, darting to the right in my direction. He blinked several times. I felt like he was asking why I had stopped, why I was leaving. I kissed my fingertips and placed them on his cheek, and then, somehow, I pulled myself up and walked away. I don't know how, and I even judge myself for being able to do it.

I cried myself to sleep that night. I cried because he was strapped to a board. I cried because I had to take my hand away from his cheek. I cried out of overwhelming emotion because I had witnessed something powerful. I *felt* it. Words were lost in translation. But there was something that transcended limitations. It was a language, not of country or ethnicity or mental capacity, but of humanity; it was the power of human touch and the potential it carries to soothe a wound deep inside a soul.

———

A few weeks later, I sat on the grass in front of a favorite fast-food restaurant for a regular Friday lunch date with a close friend, our legs stretched out before us as our tank-topped shoulders quickly bronzed in the California sun. I told her the story of my visitor from Italy/San Francisco/heaven, and she responded with appropriate wide-eyed appreciation for what he had offered to me. I said aloud what it had given me, and then in the very next sentence, self-doubt crept back in and threatened to minimize his words as I said, "But he was just some random person, I guess."

"No!" she protested passionately. "That's just it. Because everybody can be someone random to someone else." It was the randomness, and divineness of it, that made the truth so poignant. I smiled and nodded my head at what she had affirmed — both the recognition of what I had been given and of what I could give to another.

⁓

God isn't always there in the form of an answer we want or a cure we seek. But he *is* there. He is there in the power of human touch or in the power of a gracious heart that simply declares, "I'm sorry."

I sincerely hoped I could somehow hang on to this, that I could just remember. For I knew it would be challenged again, perhaps by others — for sure by myself.

chapter 15

baby steps

My overseas flight was taking off from Hartsfield International Airport in two hours. It was four o'clock in the afternoon, and I was going to be on the dreaded highway "connector" during the heart of rush-hour traffic. Atlanta is ranked number four for United States cities with the worst traffic, and anyone who has lived in my home city knows that Interstate 85 can change your temperament to the extent that by the time you reach your destination, you aren't even sure you like *yourself* anymore, much less anyone else on the road.

My brother, Nate, asked again what time my flight was and then raised his eyebrows as he glanced at the digital clock on the dashboard. I wanted to stop at my storage unit on the way, and although he didn't say a word, I knew he didn't think we had time for this. At six foot two, Nate is tall and broad shouldered. He is a big presence, but he has a patient and gentle spirit, especially with his sisters. He had flown into town only a few hours before and offered to make the hour-long drive back to where he had just come from so he could take me to the airport himself.

Without argument, he took the slight detour and pulled into the parking lot in front of several storage buildings. I jumped out of the passenger seat and quickly made my way to the door.

As I pulled it toward me, it didn't move. A plastic card with the face of a clock was suctioned to the glass. The red hands had been arranged to alert customers that the attendant would return in a half hour. My shoulders slumped in disappointment, and I walked back to the car with a feeling of defeat. Nate looked at me sympathetically and slowly started to pull out of the parking lot. Some time ago I had left all the furniture I owned there and hadn't been back since. I couldn't remember my code to get in the gate and needed the attendant to help me. My brother paused as he pulled out of the parking lot and looked at me for the go-ahead.

"Wait …" I said, bringing him to a full stop. "Do you think I could jump the fence?" I asked.

"I really don't think you should do that," he said in his typically even tone. I knew the answer to this before I asked the question.

I pulled out my BlackBerry and began pushing buttons to try to find the toll-free number for the storage company. My phone wouldn't toggle through fast enough, and again without a word, Nate found the number on his clearly superior electronic device and handed it to me.

"What is the account number?" the customer service representative asked.

"I'm not sure," I said and started to explain that I had not really planned on doing this. I had come in from out of town and didn't have my papers with me.

"No problem," she said patiently. "What phone number would it be under?" This should be a simple question, but I have lost track of all the numbers I have had in the last five years. I gave her a phone number, but it was apparently not the one I thought made the most sense to use when I opened the account.

"What is your name?" she asked. I knew the answer to this question, and this made me feel better.

A few minutes later, we were through the gate and quickly made our way down a concrete hallway with fluorescent lighting and orange garage doors. When we found the right number, Nate unlocked the padlock and raised the door to unveil all of my earthly belongings and then looked at me dubiously. The room was packed full, and I was looking for the top drawer of a nightstand. My eyes scanned the items piled to the ceiling, and miraculously I spotted what I was looking for. Stepping on a chair, I climbed on top of various pieces of furniture until my arms could fit through the rungs of my dining room chairs to reach the small knob handle on the distressed black table. I was able to open it and feel around with my hand for what I was looking for. When I didn't feel it, I shined my small flashlight into the drawer. Lip balm, a pen, and a random key that led to somewhere I couldn't remember — but the circular band was gone.

─────

After ten hours, the last box was finally brought into my new apartment and placed in the only unoccupied space on the living room floor. I locked the door behind me and turned around to survey my new home. I could only sigh and imagine the hours that lay ahead of me as I tried to locate everything in the terribly disorganized and poorly labeled boxes that carried all of my belongings. The very thought made me tired, and I quickly determined that what my aching back and frizzy hair needed most was a good shower and some sleep. With each of my moves, my mother has always made sure that at the end of the day, I had one place completely set up — my bed, with a clean set of sheets and fluffed pillows. The home may have been cluttered with furniture and piles of clothing, but on the other side was a safe and cozy haven waiting for me.

I was twenty-eight years old, and this was my fourth move in less than a year, and it was loaded with feelings of insecurity. What I wanted was to feel grounded and know who or what home was. But I was aware that I had none of these things and was actually flailing, internally and externally.

Although India was still a puppy, she seemed to feel this as well, and she hid in a corner of the closet all day while the moving chaos ensued. My new apartment was nice, but somehow, now that it was mine, it seemed much less impressive than it had before signing the papers. I had studied the floor plan sketch, as if my spatially challenged mind could conceptualize what I was looking at even a little bit. The salesperson was friendly and gave me a discount on my pet deposit, and that was pretty much all it took. I didn't even look at the apartment, but with an air of indifference that I tried to mobilize into excitement, I concluded it was perfect. It apparently overlooked a Zen garden that had flowers and a trickling fountain, and I believed it would be peaceful and relaxing. The fact that it was five floors and more than sixty steps up had not deterred me. I decided that both India and I could use the exercise.

But by the end of moving day, I seemed to be able to find problems with everything. The peaceful Zen garden was impeded by a concrete view of the parking deck, and even the sound of gurgling water through an open window at night did not have the soothing effect it should have had.

A colony of ants had invaded my kitchen, and this distressed me to an irrational degree. The water pressure was not quite up to par, and my (perhaps unhealthy) love of a scalding hot shower was met with tepid temperatures. As I carefully navigated through stacked boxes to reach the bed, India followed quietly behind me. I didn't sleep well, but morning eventually arrived.

India nudged me with her wet nose — an alarm clock I could set to the minute. I lifted the covers and pulled myself up. I located first one flip-flop, then the other, abandoned in a nearby box of clothes. I pulled my gray hooded sweatshirt over my head and descended the sixty steps for India's short morning walk. I quickly determined there was no need for a workout later in the day. We arrived at the landing, and I started to walk her over to the grassy area for what I assumed would be a simple event.

But India was overwhelmed by the new sounds and sights. Every car that passed by frightened her; every unfamiliar person threatened her sense of security. It was raining, and I was standing in my pajamas, already less than eager for the unfolding of the new day and becoming increasingly frustrated. Somehow I thought that if I gave her the commands more sharply and with an unforgiving sense of urgency, she would do what she was supposed to do, and I could go inside and get back to bed. But that would only have been true if her problem was either that she was hard of hearing or insubordinate rather than the fact that she was crippled by fear.

Another car sped past, taking the rest of India's courage, and that was it. She sprinted with unrealized agility and tried to take off. I gripped the leash firmly as it tore uncomfortably at my hand. My voice grew louder, and now I was angry. Again I gave her the command we both knew she recognized, but as an SUV roared past, she found a terror that gave her even greater strength, and she went flying off. But the leash was wrapped around my wrist, and she took me with her. For a few steps anyway. My flip-flops slipped on the wet grass; my feet went right out from under me; and I landed flat on my back without an ounce of grace.

The breath had been knocked out of me, and it took several seconds to be able to pull myself up. When I slowly got up from the ground, I stood, disheveled, my pajamas covered with mud. My hair was dripping wet; my dog was running off in the distance, her leather leash trailing behind her; and tears were streaming down my cheeks.

What a sight we must have been for the new neighbors! I weakly navigated the steady flow of traffic to cross back to the steps, where my equally drenched dog stood waiting for me, her legs shaking beneath her. Her eyes were wide with fear. I briefly knelt down to apologize to her with my eyes and pet her gently. Then I picked up the end of her leash, and we slowly climbed up the stairs.

When we stepped inside, I shut the door behind me and borrowed from its resistance to slide down to the floor, already tired from the adventures of the new day. India collapsed next to me, dropped her head onto my lap, and let out a heavy sigh. I'm not sure if I realized yet that I was looking into a mirrored image. But somehow, equally terrified, we found something to support in each other.

The next day, we got to the bottom of the steps, and I was proud of her. That was far enough for the day, and we turned around, content to call it a successful trip. The following day, we made it off the landing, and one day I think we actually made it to the edge of the grass.

I learned very quickly that impatience served no purpose whatsoever. Raising my voice at India elevated her anxiety, and it didn't give her what she needed to be able to give me what I wanted. When she was afraid, the only things that settled her and prevented the next great escape were my calm voice and a reassuring pat on the head. And I tried to get her a little closer to the goal each day.

———

I remember taking the band off. As I gently tugged it over my knuckle, it was like pulling off the most painful Band-Aid in the world, over and over again. Slowly or quickly, it was going to hurt and would expose a scar. We had not seen each other in months, and it had long since been a symbol to be misunderstood rather than a declaration of something that was true. It had represented nothing that was mine or ours for some time, but it still signified a dream, and I had struggled to let go of it long after there was nothing to wrap it around anymore.

When I finally took it off, I held it between my forefinger and thumb. It was practically weightless and so thin you couldn't pinch it without it disappearing. It still looked like a lovely piece of jewelry, but the intrinsic beauty was gone. Not knowing what to do with it, I dropped it inside the top drawer of my nightstand and closed it tightly.

Several months later, I emptied drawers into an open packing box. As I tugged open the top drawer, I was surprised to see the tiny band lying there. I wondered what to do with it and contemplated throwing it into the nearby garbage bag. Instead, I just closed the drawer and left all of its contents untouched.

At least I thought I did.

Years later, my hand groped around once again inside that drawer. Nate asked helpfully, "Is it something you really need for this trip?" He was clearly more aware of time than I was.

I didn't know what to tell him, because the truth was, I just wanted to see the ring, and I didn't know exactly why. Nate tried to help, reaching his long arm in to see if he could find it. But he, too, came up empty-handed. After we checked every drawer we could open, I stood still, as if there was another option I hadn't yet considered. He said nothing; he grew up with two sisters and knows when it is best to stay silent and let us search for a while, albeit fruitlessly.

Finally I looked up at him and nodded. I was ready to go. We walked silently back to the car, and as we pulled away, he suggested that maybe I packed it safely in a box somewhere. But I know I didn't. I know it is gone. And maybe it is for the best. It had been years now. I think I wanted to find something that acknowledged what was. It no longer represented a kind of love, but instead the life I thought I was going to have and a dream that once started to take flight. Or in truth, what was never true to the dream.

I was devastated when the story unfolded, and lost when it ended. There was a dark, blank period that I don't really remember. And then life started again, and though I made efforts to process all that had transpired, at some point I did what can deceptively seem best. Because it is easier to create a box within yourself and bury whatever your "it" is securely inside. I locked it tightly and made every attempt to forget it. It was easier that way, and it seemed to make other people more comfortable. For a while, it made me more comfortable too.

But it *did* happen, and perhaps something inside a person screams out in angry protest when we try to obliterate any part of what is a piece of ourselves and it stubbornly finds a way of spilling, or gushing, out. That much we do not get to choose. But we *do* get to choose whether it is a controlled release in which we play an active role and lay things to proper rest, or whether it becomes an enemy with which we engage in an internal battle we will not only fail to win — but the graver danger is that we will delude ourselves into thinking we can.

———

I wish I could tell you that after much persistence, India and I were completely successful with our morning trips. After a month I decided that it wasn't the right place for us and that not every battle must be fought, and with the comfort of wise words from an old country song, I decided to fold 'em.

I found a cute little house to rent with a yard for India, a stone fireplace for me, and a little more peace as we adjusted to a new home and much more.

I called my friends, and we spent a cloudy Saturday loading cars, tying a wayward mattress to the top of a truck, picking up my fallen furniture on the side of the road, battling a stubborn manual transmission, and getting soaked in the rain.

I sat in gratitude that evening at a pizza place, sounds of laughter and conversation echoing around us as we filled our empty stomachs. My friends had been there for me without asking for an explanation of why we were doing this again so soon, without a word of reproach, and without hesitation. They had found a way to love me in the pouring rain, covered with mud, when I was too scared to go in any direction.

I have not regretted that move to peace, and perhaps the fact that I transferred boxes that had not been unpacked or moved upon arrival was a sign that neither India nor I had made it home.

But standing outside in the rain with her that first morning had taught me something. She was afraid, and strong words and brute force did not serve any purpose. Sometimes taking a baby step each day is a huge stride.

⌒

As acceptance took over the space that anger had once claimed, I found healing in being able to speak of what was instead of pretending it never occurred. I uttered a name to my sister one day, and it felt foreign on my lips, but it took the shape of a kind of relief too. I cannot change the end of the story, but there was something healing about acknowledging what happened, that it was part of my life — once upon a time ago. It honored the past; it freed me to move toward a future.

I think I wanted to find the ring for the tangible reminder of what once was. It was best, it was right, that it could not be found. For what I found in the drawer was the affirmation of *what is*.

It was, but life is not bound by it; it is not what remains.

chapter 16

the flavor of extraordinary

It was February 2005, and I had spent the day on the island of Nias in Indonesia. After landing on the short airstrip, my teammates and I hopped into a van and began what is still the longest four-hour trip I have ever taken. The roads were in terrible condition after having been decimated by the tsunami six weeks before. There were no shock absorbers on the tires, and we felt the full impact of every jolt. The van inched along as our driver navigated the shattered pathway. At times we even had to step out of the van as he tediously made his way straight uphill or through a ditch or attempted to cross the remains of a bridge.

We arrived in the center of town, where there was to be a ceremony commemorating the commitment of a group of Non-Governmental Organizations (NGOs) to help rebuild houses. We did not speak the tribal language, and our understanding of the situation and daily events was limited. As the governor announced the building project to the people, faces remained expressionless. There was sparse clapping, and I wondered if the people did not entirely believe they would see it happen. They had lost their houses and all they owned; perhaps they did not want to experience again faith lost in disappointment.

As the ceremony drew to a close, dark storm clouds formed

overhead. Within minutes, the lightning flashed, just seconds before a crash of thunder, and then the sky unloaded. We wound around dirt paths and finally found an overhang. I hunched underneath with my sister, my cameraman, and a friend who directed another NGO. We were a disheveled picture, with our hair plastered to our heads, our T-shirts and cargo pants soaking wet.

After the storm, we walked around the island to survey the tsunami damage and evaluate the rebuilding potential to determine how we might be able to provide relief over a period of time. By dusk, I still didn't know where we were supposed to stay that night; whenever I inquired, I was simply assured that it would all work out. After trying to gain answers, I finally gave up and just followed instructions as they were revealed to me.

It was evening. We had left on a 6:00 a.m. chartered flight that morning, had not eaten all day, and had only swallowed a few mouthfuls of water. Our clothes were damp and did not smell very nice. We were told to pick up our backpacks and follow, so we hiked about a half mile through the debris of what used to be huts and trees. We finally reached a dock, and I surveyed the vessel we were invited to step into. It had once been painted blue, though most of the paint had chipped away. It was a small boat, with wood slats stretched across it to create a type of bench for seating. Once positioned on the slat, our legs would dangle, for there was no floor beneath them. I looked at my sister, and we mentally considered our options. There were none, so we accepted the outreached hand and settled onto the bench.

It was not comfortable, and I had no idea where we were going. But fatigue managed to claim me as we cruised along the waters, and my head dropped in sleep. I awoke to urgent dialogue back and forth. There seemed to be a problem, but I could not understand what it was. It was pitch-black now, and I couldn't see the water or my dangling feet, or anything around us. I caught sight of a small flashbulb across the way. And then finally, in English, they told us what the problem was. The tsunami had destroyed the dock on the other side. There was no way to get to shore. Rather, there was no way for the boat to get to shore.

They told us to jump in. We were going to have to wade to shore. And so we lowered ourselves into the water, holding our backpacks and the camera equipment over our heads, and followed the glowing light until we stepped up onto the sandy landing. With just a hand motion, we were directed to follow our guide. I was too tired to even try to ask questions, like where we were going and who was leading us. I had learned I would probably not hear an answer, and so I just followed. We hiked about a mile through a jungle, pushing back brush as we tried to follow down a path. We were still guided by a single light in front, and so I unsuccessfully tried to avoid branches that suddenly struck me in the face, and I stumbled clumsily on rocks or roots that protruded from the ground.

Eventually, we stepped out of our jungle and into dim light. I could hear the sound of waves crashing so I knew we were on the beach, but the light only extended a few feet out — not far enough to be able to see the water. A friendly couple from Belgium introduced themselves to us. This island was a surfer's paradise, they told us. Of course, no surfers were there at this particular time. Our hosts pointed us in the direction of a wooden shack where we would sleep for the night. They warned us that the generator would shut down in twenty minutes, and it would then be pitch-black. They offered us something to eat, but when our fatigue declined on our behalf, they said good night and closed the door behind them.

I surveyed the surroundings of this shack. Three rolled-up mats would serve as mattresses for my sister, my friend, and me. My sister and I did not have sheets or towels or clean clothes. As my friend unzipped her bag, I watched her pull out pink satin pajamas, a set of clean towels, and satin sheets. My mouth dropped open in a silent yet loaded wordless expression.

"Yes?" she asked.

I could only point to her treasure chest and then lifted my hands into the air, wondering how the nugget of information that we would need such things had somehow not passed between us.

"Sorry," she offered with a shrug of her shoulders.

I walked into the bathroom and then immediately retreated, took my sister by the hand, and led her back to the doorway.

"I don't know how to use that," I said, pointing to what was meant to be the toilet. "Please help." My vocabulary was very limited at this point.

I quickly exchanged my damp and dirty clothes for a pair of shorts and a T-shirt that had been rolled up in my bag. The generator shut off. All was dark and silent, and I drifted off to sleep.

I awoke early in the morning, not because I had gotten enough sleep, but because of the heat. Restless and not wanting to wake my friend, I got up off the mat and quietly unlatched the door. I stepped outside into a different world from the one I entered the night before.

Expanding before me was the most pristine beach I had ever seen. Shimmering blue-green water rolled up on the sand just steps from my bare feet. My night's refuge was Asu Island; total population: twenty-five people. The sun was just beginning to peek along the horizon, colors of pink and yellow streaking across the sky. No one had yet stirred, and the beach was empty — and it was breathtaking in its natural, uncorrupted beauty. I stepped onto powdery white sand soft as sugar and walked gingerly toward the water. I found myself tiptoeing, as if I would disrupt the perfection if I moved too quickly. After dipping my toes in to test the temperature, I found a place on the sand to sit and watch the sky open in color — shades of orange and red — from my perfectly isolated seat. The water continued to draw up gently onto the shore, barely reaching my toes and trickling back down.

It was my birthday. I was in the exact same place as the night before, but in the darkness I found nothing beautiful about the surroundings and resented its very existence, especially the fact that it was where *I* existed at that point in time.

But in daylight, it was nothing short of paradise. The setting was exactly the same. The single thing that changed with the morning light was *my perspective.*

———

I have long held an adoration for Italy, and as the deadline for my manuscript inched ever closer, it seemed like the perfect time for a retreat to a setting that is positively inspiring. This idea evolved into a month-long trip, which evolved into moving out of my apartment to save the rent money, which evolved into selling all of my furniture to avoid storage. My possessions and home were contained in my car and parked in someone's driveway in San Diego.

I found what I was looking for in Italy; I found what I didn't know I was looking for in Italy. Tucked away in a flat that was part of a quaint farmhouse outside of Siena, I wrapped myself in a gray wool sweater and fleece-lined yoga pants and sat in the middle of a garden in Tuscany. I carefully opened my laptop when I arrived, and with a deep breath, I began lightly tapping the black keys to leave the anonymity and safety of my own thoughts and put them to the permanence of paper instead.

I loved it there, and as soon as I arrived I wished I did not have to leave. I loved the woman in the cheese shop who gave me sample after sample before I decided on a particular Pecorino. I loved the sweet older man in the flower shop off the piazza who carefully wrapped my yellow and red gerbera daisies. I loved sipping cappuccino at an outdoor café where I sat for hours each day and was never asked to leave. I loved looking up and seeing amazingly picturesque architecture, even lamp shades of streetlights that were no less than a work of art.

I know that all of this still had a halo of idealism, since it was new, but when I hung laundry on a line outside to be dried by the morning sun, I felt like I was in the middle of a Bounce commercial. I didn't know a soul, so when I heard a knock on the door, I knew it was my only consistent visitor, a sweet lady who doesn't know I have adopted her as my nonna. She didn't speak a word of English, and my knowledge of Italian had been fairly exhausted when we said, "Buon giorno." She would grin as she handed me a bowl of steaming pasta with homemade pesto, or bruschetta on fresh, warm bread decorated with bright red tomatoes. I opened my mouth with glee, exaggerating every sign of body language to compensate for the words I could not express. She put her hands to her face and looked at me with worry and said, "Sola ... sola," as she shook her head. I laughed and pulled her latest culinary creation to my heart, assuring her it would keep me plenty warm. And I meant it. We would gesture wildly for a few minutes, and then I offered up my other vocabulary word — "Ciao" — to bid her good-bye as she walked down the gravel path to her home.

After two weeks, I took an overnight trip to a town outside of Florence called San Casciano, where the friend of a friend lived.

They were gracious enough to invite me to visit, and as I hopped on bus number three of three, I looked out the window in awe of the vineyards of wine and olive oil, honey-colored villas with grasshopper-green shutters that I dreamed of buying and settling into, and the sun dropping behind rolling hills and cypress trees. It was magnificent.

When I first walked into their home at dusk, a fire was beginning to blaze in the fireplace and the kitchen was a bakery with an open bag of flour, rolling pins, dough, and brewing tea. I met "Zio," who instantly won my affection with his salt-and-pepper hair, gentle eyes, and mischievous grin. Our communication was limited because of the language barrier, but I felt like he was the cool uncle you always wanted to have, the one who spoils you and tells you that boys who don't like you are fools. Twin toddlers played a game of hide-and-seek with their six-year-old brother. The same hiding place worked like a charm. Every single time.

The owner of the house, Giovanni, shook my hand and said, "Would you like to see my safe?"

"Absolutely," I answered, having no idea what was stored there.

"It is for the wine," he answered my unspoken confusion.

"Absolutely," I confirmed, with great conviction, knowing a rich experience full of life application lay within this safe. Giovanni is a contadino, an Italian farmer who cultivates a vineyard to yield sangiovese grapes for Chianti, and an olive grove for a ripe harvest to produce olive oil. He took me downstairs into the basement, where steel vats contained white, red, or rosé wine.

"If you want to have a vineyard, you must wait three years for the grapes," he began. I already liked the process as it applied to the story of wine. I wondered why it is that when it comes to things, we can find the patience to allow time for them to grow into something; with people, and with ourselves, it is infinitely more complicated.

Giovanni explained the grape harvest and talked about the days when they were crushed with bare feet. Now a machine does this with greater efficiency, though it is far less picturesque. The machine, or a gathering of feet, squeezes the juice contained inside the skin. The skins are separated but not removed. They need the moisture from the juice to prevent them from drying out, and they have not yet finished serving their purpose of providing the rich color. The juice is then poured into barrels, with the skins floating to the top. Within hours, tiny bubbles begin to swirl into the fermentation process.

Giovanni motioned for me to lean close to a large plastic container filled with juice. If he wanted rosé wine, the grape skins are removed in a few days. For a luscious red, the skins remain a while longer to infuse their color into the juice.

"If the container is not strong, the wine will explode during the fermentation process," he said. "This is why Jesus said, 'Do not pour new wine into old wineskins.' The old skin is a little bit worn; it cannot handle the force of fermentation, and it will break." The barrels today have a narrow cylinder at the top that allows air to escape, and thus creates necessary space for the wine to breathe, but prevents air from entering and compromising the delicate balance.

After fermentation, lees — deposits of yeast — create sediment in the bottom of a vat of wine. Giovanni guided me over to another container and pointed to the distinct line along the bottom. "Now I must transfer the wine into a new container and leave the sediment behind. The sediment is a natural part of the process, but it is bitter. If it remains too long, it will not improve the flavor but will make the wine bitter." The lees will affect and enhance flavor up to a certain point, so the kind of wine desired in production determines when wine is separated from the bitter sediment. And so, under the watchful eye of the contadino, the wine is transferred into a fresh container to preserve the flavor.

When the skins are ultimately removed, they are not thrown away. "You think they are finished, that there is no more juice inside of them, but there is," he explained. The skins are squeezed carefully again, this time by a press that knows the right shape and pressure, rendering more juice that will become wine.

"In the book of Philippians, Paul says that every knee will bow and every tongue will confess. How can it be so? There are many people who, if you say to them, 'You are created by God to bring glory to him' — they will say it isn't so. They don't believe. They will not give him any glory. And it seems there is nothing we can do. But they are like these skins. If you squeeze them with your hands, nothing will come out. It seems finished. But when faced with the Creator they will spring forth with rich juice because they are made in his image; they cannot help but reflect his image. Like this, every knee will bow and every tongue will confess that Jesus Christ is Lord."

Pulling a stemmed glass from the shelf, Giovanni asked, "So which one would you like to try?" I picked red, and he poured a little bit of wine into the glass, straight from a spout in the vat. It had not completed the fermentation process, and while it definitely tasted like a kind of wine, it was light in flavor and color.

"Some people like it this way, even prefer it," he said. "But a real wine expert would know that it was not yet finished."

We were then called upstairs to dinner — a spread of prosciutto, arugula, fresh mozzarella, and piadine, an ancient Italian unleavened flatbread. For dessert, creamy Nutella was generously spread between two slices of fresh piadine, the warmth from the bread melting the chocolate layer of the sandwich perfectly. Carafes of red wine sat on the farm table as fifteen of us gathered around. The wine looked even prettier to me when I understood where it had come from and what it had come through.

Sometime after midnight, we sipped the last of the espresso; the soccer game on TV ended for its fans; and we said good night and allowed "Zio" the privacy of the living room to fall asleep on the sofa that would be his bed. I went to my room for the night, changed into my pajamas, and retrieved a book from my bag for a little nighttime reading — *Italian for Beginners*. I pulled my fleece over my head and walked to the window by the bed and drew back the linen curtain. I knew that on the other side of the window was a beautiful vineyard, but it lay hidden in the darkness of night. I let the curtain fall back in place and crawled underneath the wonderful layers of blankets. I wanted to remember everything Giovanni had said, because it had rich meaning for me.

I found it purposeful that the sediment was there at all, that bitter yeast was necessary for fermentation, and that it served a purpose for a time. Without the knowledge of the process necessary to achieve flavor, an amateur would mistakenly conclude that a bitter taste should be removed immediately or avoided altogether. But this wasn't the case. The sediment was part of a necessary process, and the wine was not immediately relieved of its bitterness by the contadino. The process required the careful eye of one who knew when enough time had gone by, when the presence of sediment no longer served to enhance but would instead destroy — but one who also knew enough to risk the presence and potential of something bitter, for its proportion made the flavor true. And within its truth lay the texture and richness that was the very character of the wine itself, the difference between a good wine and one that is legendary.

I have been thinking about my life quite a bit lately, the parts that I wish were not there, the places that still ache. While I do not believe that God caused the harsh things to happen, I do think he allowed them. The bitter thus far has been potent, and at times it seemed to threaten to ruin the flavor altogether. At times, I thought it was ruined. Perhaps, like a contadino, God's watchful eye was on me, and he allowed that which was painfully bitter to infuse something purposeful. Somehow, believing that he would have intervened and said, "Enough," if it was going to destroy me — or that perhaps he *did* do that — seemed comforting.

I am not in a place where I can say I am grateful for all that has happened. Given the choice I still wish very much that it could have been different, that there had been another way to have learned the lessons. I struggle to accept the life that is mine because it is not the story that I wanted. And not a day goes by that I don't notice it still hurts inside.

But I *can* say that if I had to choose between who I was before and who I am now, without being able to alter the path of events, I would pick the now, even with all that it carries. Life was simpler before; I didn't carry some of the same sensitivities, and there weren't the same relational land mines another could unknowingly step into. But now I see the world with perspective; I view people through vastly different lenses and recognize beauty in things that once escaped my notice. God seems more mysterious — sometimes mysteriously confusing, absent, and maddening. But always mysteriously true. If I am honest, life is ever more complicated but undeniably richer.

The truth is, I didn't really like the taste of the wine that had not endured a process. It didn't taste bad. It was just … forget-table. I can tell you what it lacked more than I can articulate what it contained. It lacked fullness and substance and something that made you savor the very essence of a sip even as it trickled down your throat. I tasted the wine that was a deep shade of burgundy velvet — the wine that had undergone the process of fermenta-tion in which sediment had formed and been filtered and skins had fully infused their color, the wine that had accepted the gift of time until it was ready to be tasted — and it was a sip of the extraordinary. Given the choice, I would opt for a life that is extraordinary over a life that is simple. Perhaps I was not meant to be a simple girl.

When I awoke in the morning, I pulled back the blankets and stood at the window again. I drew back the curtain, and an audi-ble breath escaped my lips. The morning light revealed a spectac-ularly beautiful vineyard that stretched as far as I could see. Even though it was the beginning of winter and I was not viewing the vines in their fullness, as in the season of harvest — even so, the sunlight revealed that I looked upon signs of vintage glory.

chapter 17

a complete vision

In *The Agony and the Ecstasy,* a young Michelangelo was debating with his friends about whether the superior art form was painting or sculpture. It must be, without a doubt, painting, his friends insisted. Sculpture was monotonous and limited, they claimed. After all, the painter could portray the entire universe; her skill required the creativity and skill to create the illusion of a third dimension, as well as foresight to anticipate the final result of color and design within the canvas of fresh, wet plaster.

But Michelangelo fought back tears, surprised by the intensity of emotion in his reaction. Sculpture came closer to true form; it was three-dimensional. And didn't art only become noble to the degree to which it represented the truth? he rhetorically asked. "If a painter blundered, what did he do? He patched and repaired and covered over with another layer of paint. The sculptor on the contrary had to see within the marble the form that it held. He could not glue back broken parts. That was why there were no more sculptors today, because it took a thousand times more accuracy of judgment and vision."[13]

Much to my dismay, I am not one who can create art; I can only appreciate its beauty. But when I read this passage, I was intrigued to understand more. I called a friend who is part of a family of artists, and she put me in touch with her mother. An accomplished painter, her words of explanation brought tears to my eyes. It is true, she told me. The painter has the option to rethink, to reconsider his direction, his statement, his intensity, his heart left on the canvas for the world to see.

But a sculptor must work with inspired insight. The vision of the end must be complete before he ever begins. "The first blows of his chisel cannot be gentle, and in their harshness they must be accurate," she explained. There are no do-overs for a sculptor. If he errs, the marble can either become a new creation or remain a lifeless shard of stone. But it cannot return to what it was. It can be shaped into something new. Ever different in form, but ever true to its essence.

As my friend described this process, emotions stirred within me as I realized with gratitude that God is the Master Sculptor. He is concerned about the essence of who we are — the form that we have — and the masterpiece is the outcome of that essence in the capable hands of the Artist and Visionary.

But there is another question. God as the Sculptor allows us to be his art. But what of *our* hands? How will *we* live to create? Will we be painters who cover up mistakes with a new stroke or different color to distract from the error? This is easier. It takes less time, and we don't have to change the overall image for anyone to see. *The relationship broke?* It's easier to slap on a Band-Aid and find a new relationship instead of taking time to grieve its loss. *You failed and fell?* It's easier to draw broad strokes *over* it so no one can testify to it.

But if we are to have vision, will we instead see others and even ourselves in the same way a sculptor sees marble — a sculptor who knows that she cannot just cover it up and put it all back together as if it was never fractured? Instead, she knows that to have it restored, she has to have insight for what it can wholly become — something different but ever faithful to its essence. It will never be what it was, for its nature is too rich to be patched up. But the eye of a sculptor looks into the form of the marble and knows that the guided chisel can shape it into something. Not as it was before, but uncompromisingly true to its essence, and lovely.

———

Mariam had left Amman, Jordan, with her husband, Rayan, and their two small children to minister in Europe. The country that would be their temporary home was beautiful, with soaring snow-capped mountains and an abundance of schnitzel.

Rayan loved to climb, and his dark eyes danced excitedly as he recounted an epic experience to his wife one evening. She *had* to climb this mountain, he said. The view is *spectacular*, he all but whispered to emphasize its inexplicable delight.

Some months later, a group of people arrived to visit them. Rayan was taking them on his favorite climb, and he implored Mariam to go with them. Given her responsibilities for two small children, her days were long and filled with things to do — things that consumed great energy. She was not used to climbing and knew it would be difficult. But she could not resist the lure of the gleam in his eyes that day when he told her of the beauty of the views, a beauty he wanted to share with her.

With the help of a nanny, she began the intense, physically demanding climb that would render breathtaking rewards in the end. But halfway through, her body pleaded for sensible relief. She stopped to rest, and her concerned husband released her from any pressure she might have felt. "I can't stay," he explained. "I have to lead the rest of the group up the mountain. But stay here and rest, and we will find you on our way down," he assured her.

And so she watched Rayan and the group disappear from sight. As she regained steady breathing, her calf muscles still cried out in protest of even the thought of movement.

The view is spectacular. She did not want to miss seeing what he had described, what had affected him so much; she wanted to witness unspeakable beauty. And so she shook her head at the aches and fatigue and began to ascend the mountain.

Her lungs struggled to match the task, and her feet ached, but her mind was determined. And as she made it to the mountain peak and arrived at the edge of beautiful, she saw Rayan in the distance. Even from afar, she could see the smile of pride on his face. He left the side of a companion and ran toward his wife. "I knew you would come!"

Placing his hands on her shoulders to steady her breathing, he repeated, "I knew you would come. I told them, 'If I know my wife, she won't give up. She'll keep on climbing because she knows that the view from the top is amazing.'"

Rayan was her greatest champion, the person who gave her the kind of irreplaceable place we all long for. And when he cried out in pain from a fierce headache, she prayed and prayed, believing that God would heal her husband from this inexplicable ailment. She sat by the hospital bed, accompanied by her unusually large extended family. They were certain he would get better soon.

But that is not how his story ended, and only days later, Mariam found herself dressed in black, with a lace head covering shielding her eyes from unobstructed view. He was gone. The one person who knew her and loved her completely was gone. She was a widow — and a single mother.

"Your ministry was with Rayan. And he is gone," Mariam was told as she was gently released from her role. She had lost her husband and her safe place in life, and now she was losing her place in ministry. Tears of sadness were replaced by tears of anger. Why had God done this to her? Why had he taken so much?

She kept up a facade for her children that evening and kissed their foreheads as she tucked them into bed. And then she crawled into the respite of her own cool sheets. She sobbed into her pillow, feeling tired and helpless. It was too much. She didn't know how to continue without Rayan. She didn't know if she wanted to. But frankly, she was angry with him too. Everything hurt, and the fatigue of her spirit and the ache in her heart beckoned her to give up. "How could you leave me like this? How could you leave me to walk alone? Where *are* you?" she passionately cried aloud to the husband who was not lying beside her.

And then, in the quiet afforded by the inhale of a sob, she heard his voice.

If I know my wife, she won't give up. She'll keep on climbing because she knows that the view from the top is amazing.

chapter 18

a fairy tale

This is a story from my life, one I started to see unfold when I walked into an unlikely room to listen to the story of another. It continued when I stepped over goats and cows and garbage to visit smiling children living in a shelter on a dark and grievous street in Bombay. It deepened when I stood on a deserted beach littered with devastation and unspeakable loss from a cruel tsunami. It offered freedom when I let a friend into the dark places that filled me with shame and fear — and I was met by him with grace.

I thought I was running *from* something. As it turns out, I was running *toward* something.

In the presence of things that were broken — dreams, intentions, ambitions, and human spirit — I found invaluable lessons about life in the vulnerability of Annie, and her convicting questions; the integrity of grief and acceptance of Anna; the angst and perseverance of Mariam. These are present-day examples of age-old stories. These people have not established my belief in whom or what God uses; they were just revelations in real time of what he had already told me.

Our biblical heroes include Moses, who killed an Egyptian and then wandered the desert for forty years to flee the wrath of

Pharaoh. When God called him to carry out his plan to free the Israelites, Moses doubted both his worthiness and his physical ability to effectively do the job. But through Moses, God would eventually bring the Israelites to the Promised Land. He would invite Moses to Mount Sinai and deliver to him stone tablets of laws written by the finger of God. He would allow Moses to see his glory, not the face that no man could look upon, but the back of the living God as he passed by.

Then there was Peter, a disciple who was specifically and literally called by Jesus, who heard him teach and witnessed his miracles. And when Jesus was unjustly imprisoned and awaiting a death sentence, Peter disowned his master and friend in an act of scathing betrayal. Not once, but three times. Yet the one who knew that Peter would do this changed his name from Simon to Cephas, an Aramaic name for Peter that means "rock." "And I tell you, you are Peter, and on this rock I will build my church" (Matthew 16:18). Jesus knew that Peter would follow him. He knew that Peter would disown him. He knew that Peter would live for him, and he knew that one day Peter would die for him. Peter was prophetically named not for his would-be failures; he was named for his genuine strength of heart.

The biblical heroes also include Rahab, a woman who worked in a brothel. She would have been content to receive just a bread crumb from Jesus and was ultimately recognized for her faith. The Messiah would come, not through what we might think an obvious choice — a "reputable" woman — but through the bloodline of a woman who had been a prostitute.

We tend to romanticize and glorify personalities decades later, but I think even the heroes of our faith would be quick to remind us of the details we forget, the price of evil that was demonstrated even in their own choices and lives. When I look back at history, it is evident that God has always worked through flawed individuals.

To our own loss, as we do with fairy tales, we forget the flaws and the manifestations of evil and the great cost it had to each one. And there is an unintended act of grace in this. It reveals that these flaws did not define them or their story. In this way, our memory displays greater insight than our conscious mind. These heroes were more than the sum of their failures, more than the horrific things done to them or the heinous things done by them. We remember the glory, the acts of heroic proportion. We want to identify with the hero; we forget we can all identify with the flaws too. And yet in the world around us, we so easily exchange this perspective to levy on an individual the fine he or she has earned.

Interestingly enough, Jesus reserved his strongest words not for the unwed mother, the woman in prostitution, the one who committed adultery, the one who is divorced, and all those who wear obvious and great scarlet letters of moral failure. And interestingly enough, Satan did not fall from heaven for any of those reasons; the fallen angel descended from the heights of heaven because of pride. Jesus saved his strongest words for the self-righteous, for it was the heart of an individual that earned his concern. The truth is that we are all flawed and in need of redemption, of the grandest rescue. And the miracle is that he brings beauty not in spite of but through our flaws.

So does it follow that pain and heartache are the only way to discover life, to find meaning? I cannot say that it isn't possible without it; I don't pretend to have that kind of supernatural insight. What I can say is that I wanted a life that was enchanting and flawless — but both are not possible. The Bible tells me so; life taught me so; even the fairy tales warned me that this was so.

I'm thankful my life is the way it is, and I know it was not by chance. God offered me the opportunity to grow into something and was willing to forgo the ease for what is the greater dream. And so am I.

Life is about fighting through what is painful, what is down-right wrong, for the sake of what is right. And it is about treasuring the moments and the experiences that make living undeniably special and the everyday miraculous. Some days, we can see it in our own lives; other days, witnessing the miraculous in the life of another can be enough until we find it again in our own.

> For there is hope for a tree....
> Though its root grow old in the earth,
>   and its stump die in the soil,
> yet at the scent of water it will bud
>   and put out branches like a young plant.
>
> JOB 14:7–9

When your leaves have fallen in crumbles, no longer providing shade for others or yourself; when there are no blooms on your branches; when you are stripped of the branches themselves that once gave perceived heavenly height and balance; when you are but a stump that has died in the ground, you do little more than take up space. You don't bring fruit, beauty, or canopy but are something to stumble over or stub a toe on, something to be altogether ignored. Life has essentially abandoned you.

Unless, until, there is water. No ... the promise is that at even the *scent* of water, our roots, like that of a tree, will awaken and extend themselves — at the very *hint* of its refreshment and sustenance. Ah, the perfume of hope that breathes life into the weary and wounded.

And life is discovered in spite of, because of, what remained.

Sometimes a discovery follows an intense and deliberate search; and then there are those priceless moments when it arrives unexpectedly and is placed in the palm of your hand.

One month in Italy passed by quickly, and it is with nostalgia that I prepare to pack my bags and return home in just a short week's time.

There is a café in the town square of Siena. It is here I sat every day at the same table, in the same chair, looking at the same view. It is now the day before Thanksgiving, and the unseasonable warmth from the sun has given way to a cool, crisp evening as the moon beamed over the top of the historic town hall building. I was sipping the last of a cappuccino after hours of hovering over my laptop. To my great confusion, when I lowered my coffee cup, I was face-to-face with an Italian young man, standing beside me with a beautiful yellow gerbera daisy in his hand.

"It is for you," he said as he presented the flower to me. I sat up in my seat and looked behind me to the someone else he must have been speaking to. When I realized there was no one else, I shook my head no. It couldn't be for me. But he placed it in my hesitant hand, smiled, and quickly disappeared.

I looked up at Franco, the gentleman who had brought countless frothy cappuccinos and plates of bread and cheese to my table in the last several days. He spoke a bit of English, and so I tried to explain to him, "I don't think this is for me."

He disagreed, smiled, and asked, "You have a friend in Florence, no?" I started to shake my head, but I stopped suddenly, with a look of uncertainty. Franco suggested that I would find an answer in the small card I had failed to notice was tucked inside the folds of tissue paper. I carefully opened a vanilla-colored envelope to retrieve a priceless note.

As I absorbed the scripted message, I instantly sat up and looked all around, but there was no sign of the face that had recently grown familiar. Deep down inside, I knew this face was, in fact, several miles away. I had not planned it; I wasn't looking for it. In fact, I had been certain I didn't even want it any more. I thought that this part of me had died, and I had mourned its passing.

A soft light descended on the piazza and illuminated the grand clock that was recording time as I looked at the surrounding balconies and red bricks that could tell of countless conversations and history. The rhythm of the Italian language in nearby murmurings provided a musical score, and an older gentleman sitting at a nearby café table watched both my gift and confusion with amused curiosity.

I slowly settled back into my chair, broke into a grin, and brought the flower gently to my lips and inhaled deeply. The sky of midnight blue was bright with gems I knew by name, and I sat, fully present, beneath its total expanse.

I felt the distinct sensation of something awakening within me. It was not that something lost had been found. Something new was being uncovered, discovered. I did not know what my future held, yet of this I could be sure: It would include some things messy with painful thorns, some things sweet with a taste to savor, all things rich. For today, it held a single yellow gerbera daisy. I carefully wrapped my hand around its stem to cling to it tightly.

———

Still climbing ... because the view from the top is amazing.
And they all lived ... ever after.

Jacoline's story

Let me first give you a glimpse at the beginning of my story, so you can understand what today means.

I was born in South Africa, the second of two girls. My father was an alcoholic, and my mother a bit of a wreck due to it. My sister and I grew up in Malawi, very beautiful and innocent. My father died when I was eight years old and my sister was nine. We left Malawi and traveled back to South Africa, as we had cousins there. I remember it being quite a culture shock, and our long dresses and long socks were quickly changed for short skirts and socks rolled down to fit in with all the cool kids. That's when a lot of my problems started. My mother remarried, and my step-father was not a good man. As I got older, my sister and I started going to clubs, and I began drinking and smoking marijuana at the age of fourteen.

My mom was not strong and made it clear we were a burden to her. I had a dream to be an English teacher, as I excelled in academics, particularly in English. I applied for a bursary award for university and managed to get in. But I was partying heavily at this stage and ended up dropping out of school and waitressing full-time for many years.

I remember arriving in Cape Town with nothing but the clothes on my back. I saw an ad for an escort agency job in which you needed no experience and could make fast money. I naively believed I would truly just be escorting men to dinners. What a fool I was! They quickly told me what the job actually entailed, and I hightailed it out of there. But I couldn't find a job, and so I applied again as an escort, knowing what I was getting into. I convinced myself that I would work for a couple of weeks, just to get on my feet. But I got trapped by the easy money, and you begin to think that this is just who you are now — a prostitute. How do you go back to being normal?

I met my husband while I was working as an escort. I thought he was going to save me from all of it. We boarded a plane to London, and I was in a foreign country when I realized he was expecting me to use my trade there to support him. He began drinking heavily and became abusive all the time while I was sleeping with other men and bringing money home to him. I despised him for ruining all of my dreams of marriage and romance.

I soon became pregnant, but ran away from my husband while my child was still young. I was tired of his drinking, of the abuse. I left to protect myself and my daughter. But I had a drug habit and a child to support, so I continued to sell myself for many years. My drugging got worse, and I eventually could not support my daughter and had to give her away. My life spiraled badly after that. I had another child — a son — and I lost him too because I could not care for him.

One night on the streets, a woman offered me a warm house to stay in. She spoke of a God who she was confident loved me and saw me, in spite of everything. I had been desperate. My life was a disaster. I did not know how to change my circumstances, but I knew my heart wanted to change. I grabbed the offer but kept slipping back until eventually I got down on my knees and told God this was it — I was giving it my all.

I wasn't sure if I should dare to dream, but I knew I was discovering things I loved. I dreamed of a future, of being a chef and working in a real job and being successful. Shortly afterward, I met Naomi and became aware of Wellspring International. She was visiting South Africa and came to the home where I was staying. She asked what my dream job would be, and I knew the answer immediately. At the time I didn't really know who they were or what they did. We were just talking, and it was comfortable.

Soon afterward, Wellspring offered to pay for my studies at culinary school. I gave it my all and came in first in the class! I now had an identity as a chef instead of a prostitute. Do you understand what this means? I got a job at a high-class restaurant in Cape Town. And a scooter to get to work. I loved riding that scooter — it was the first thing I owned. I loved feeling the wind in my face as I drove to work and back to my home at night. Wellspring also helped me get my son back and paid some of our rent and a portion of the tuition for his education, while I paid the rest of our expenses with my salary.

That was five years ago. Just a few months ago, Wellspring helped me open my own restaurant. This restaurant — it's my little baby. I picked every paint color. I created a menu. I even designed the aprons. I can't decide if I want to laugh or cry when I think of it. Who would have ever thought I would be here? From the street, from the gutter, to my dream. I want to use this to honor God. I love this dream, this restaurant, because I look at all the wonderful foods he has given us to sustain us and keep us healthy. I want to help people learn to be healthy and take care of their bodies. It's an important job. Food is an amazing gift. It should be enjoyed and celebrated and used to make us stronger. That's what this restaurant is for.

Wellspring gave me a second chance, and I am living a changed life. I am free. I am proud of myself. And my children are proud of me. Now for the first time in my life, I see my daughter looking at me with pride. That makes everything worth it. She is fifteen now and just spent the summer working at my restaurant with me. It's the first time I have really spent time with her — working in my restaurant and teaching her. My son, who is now twelve, has been with me for six years and is doing well. Each day he brings a group of friends home from school. They come into our restaurant in their gray uniforms and ties, dragging their backpacks with them, and march back to the kitchen to place orders for after-school snacks. This way I make sure they are eating healthy foods instead of junk food. They sit at tables and play games or go hang out in our little one-room apartment in the back. It makes me happy that they want to be here. I'm the "cool" mom — do you know that? My son's friends think it's so cool that he lives here, that his mom has this restaurant, that we can make them something good to eat.

A new business isn't easy and I have to work so hard. It is scary sometimes, but I am learning to work hard, to continue to believe in a future.

No one can tell me there is not a God. He didn't give up on me. He has given me my own restaurant. I have a family. I am not ashamed of my story. I will tell it to anyone who will listen. My story only matters — I only matter — when you understand where I have come from and the story and power of redemption. All the people along the way — I want to make them proud and thank them for putting their faith in me.

For them, for my children, for God ... I will succeed.

acknowledgments

Author Anne Lamott has said, "Almost all good writing begins with terrible first efforts. You need to start somewhere." For some of us, it takes more than a first effort, and ultimately it is the cavalry of support alongside that enables you, and it, to survive. My sincere gratitude and appreciation to each of them:

To the people in these stories, for allowing me to step into your lives and awaken my own.

To my agent, Erik Wolgemuth, dependable, professional, and always the advocate.

To my editor, Angela Scheff, who was the first to encourage me to write. And then painstakingly went through it all to make it ever better.

To Katy, for Friday lunch dates and being a faithful sounding board.

To my family: Mom, Dad, Sarah, and Nathan, for being the best family in the world by a vote of 5 to nothing; to Alan and SJ, for making it 8 and true.

And finally, to my husband, Drew, for making my project his passion, for reading it more times than I have — out loud, backward, and upside down — for bringing me lattes, granting me patience, engaging in my angst over a single word ... and showing me that, somehow, I seem to have a fan, book or not. I am head over heels.

notes

1. G. K. Chesterton, *Orthodoxy* (New York: Kessinger, 2004), 30–45.

2. Irving Stone, *The Agony and the Ecstasy* (New York: Penguin, 1987), 79.

3. Jean Shinoda Bolen, *Goddesses in Everywoman* (New York: HarperCollins, 2004), 1–2.

4. J. R. R. Tolkien, *The Fellowship of the Ring*: *Being the First Part of* The Lord of the Rings (New York: HarperCollins, 2001), 224.

5. F. W. Boreham, *Dreams at Sunset* (London: Epworth, 1954), 93.

6. Irving Stone, *The Agony and the Ecstasy* (New York: Penguin, 1987), 48.

7. Stone, *Agony and Ecstasy*, 48.

8. C. S. Lewis, *A Grief Observed* (New York: Seabury, 1961), 47.

9. Gregory David Roberts, *Shantaram* (New York: Macmillan, 2005), 387.

10. Paulo Coelho, *The Witch of Portobello* (New York: HarperCollins, 2007), 44.

11. Coelho, *Witch of Portobello*, 45.

12. Coelho, *Witch of Portobello*, 46.

13. Irving Stone, *The Agony and the Ecstasy* (New York: Penguin, 1987), 40.

Share Your Thoughts

With the Author: Your comments will be forwarded to the author when you send them to zauthor@zondervan.com.

With Zondervan: Submit your review of this book by writing to zreview@zondervan.com.

Free Online Resources at

www.zondervan.com

Zondervan AuthorTracker: Be notified whenever your favorite authors publish new books, go on tour, or post an update about what's happening in their lives at www.zondervan.com/authortracker.

Daily Bible Verses and Devotions: Enrich your life with daily Bible verses or devotions that help you start every morning focused on God. Visit www.zondervan.com/newsletters.

Free Email Publications: Sign up for newsletters on Christian living, academic resources, church ministry, fiction, children's resources, and more. Visit www.zondervan.com/newsletters.

Zondervan Bible Search: Find and compare Bible passages in a variety of translations at www.zondervanbiblesearch.com.

Other Benefits: Register yourself to receive online benefits like coupons and special offers, or to participate in research.

ZONDERVAN.com/
AUTHORTRACKER
follow your favorite authors

Wellspring International assists individuals in need and existing organizations serving women and children at risk. Our mission is to provide a holistic response to the physical, emotional, and spiritual needs we encounter and to empower donors to make informed decisions about their giving and participation in a broken world that longs for hope.

RE-ENTRY
RESTORATION
REHABILITATION
RESCUE

We have the opportunity to aid organizations who embody **FOUR** aspects we believe are vital to this ministry:

wellspring international
an outreach of RZIM